Do-It-Yourself Decorating

Step-by-Step
Wall Tiling

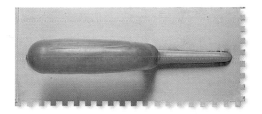

Alex Portelli

Meredith® Press

Des Moines, Iowa

Contents

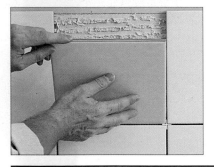

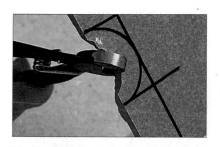
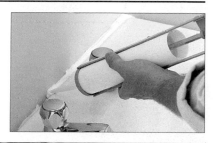

Introduction

Ceramic wall tiles have been used for centuries; there's no better testimony to their usefulness and durability. Despite the advent of other more modern materials, the glazed clay tile is still the most practical way to give a wall an attractive, easy-to-clean, hard-wearing, waterproof surface that will keep its appearance for years to come. These qualities are essential in bathrooms and kitchens, but also are much appreciated in laundry and utility rooms.

In recent years, there's been a steady increase in the number of people who are willing to tackle home improvement jobs themselves rather than hire professionals. Responding to this trend, suppliers and manufacturers have made materials and tools designed for the amateur rather than the professional, often simplifying the work in the process. This, in turn, has encouraged even more homeowners to do it themselves.

Tiling, however, isn't quite as simple as it seems. Getting a professional finish takes a fair amount of skill. That's not to say that amateurs can't achieve good results—it just takes care and patience and an understanding of what you're doing and why.

The following chapters will show you all the techniques and tips you need to successfully tile a wall. If you use the information in this book and take your time, there's no reason you can't achieve long-lasting results that make you proud.

Ideas and Choices

There's a world of wall tiles to choose from in a wide range of colors, patterns, textures, and sizes. Most are ceramic, but you also can find marble tiles and mosaics in a variety of other materials. As a result, no matter what the style of your bathroom, kitchen, laundry room, or utility room, you'll be able to find the right tiles for the job.

Take your time when choosing your tiles; tiles are not only more expensive than other wall treatments, but they're also harder to change if you want to redecorate. It's important to find a color and pattern you'll be happy with for a long time. If you're in doubt, opt for something simple that will provide a neutral backdrop rather than a design that will become a major decorating element in the room. You'll find additional inspiration in magazines, other people's homes, tile brochures, displays at tile outlets, and even the patterns in wallpaper and fabric.

Classical influence

The use of tiles and mosaics in bathrooms dates back many centuries. They're the most practical materials to give walls—as well as floors—an attractive, waterproof surface. Combined with carefully chosen bathroom fixtures, they give a bathroom a timeless, classical look.

One important consideration, regardless of the style of your bathroom, is to use large tiles when tiling a large area such as a wall or even a complete room. Large tiles will give you a less busy-looking surface, and in a small room, they actually may help it look larger. Reserve small tiles such as mosaics for backsplashes and other small areas.

◄ Although popular bathroom color schemes continually come into and go out of fashion, white fixtures and white tiles never seem to date. Still, a large expanse of white tiles looks cold and uninteresting; you need to add some sort of accent to create a focal point. In this particular case, the walls were divided into horizontal panels by contrasting rows of tiles in blues and grays.

At waist height, a dado was formed by adding a row of patterned tiles designed just for this purpose. They're the same size as the field tiles, making layout easy (see pages 32–35). Up to dado height, the field tiles are set conventionally and are aligned both horizontally and vertically. Above the dado, though, the rows run diagonally to create a diamond pattern.

This pattern continues up to "picture-rail" height, where a darker band of tiles provides more contrast. The design consists of narrow, dark blue pencil tiles; a row of alternating, small dark blue and white tiles; and a row of blue molded dado tiles. Above this picture rail, the white tiles continue to the ceiling in a conventional pattern.

At floor level, the picture rail is echoed by a row of pencil tiles and a row of small blue and white tiles.

Using horizontal accents this way not only breaks up a large expanse of tiles, but also lets you change the layout pattern (on part of the wall) for even more interest.

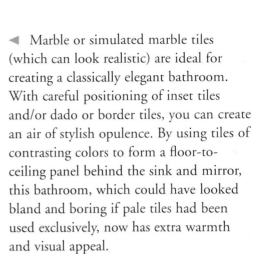

◄ Marble or simulated marble tiles (which can look realistic) are ideal for creating a classically elegant bathroom. With careful positioning of inset tiles and/or dado or border tiles, you can create an air of stylish opulence. By using tiles of contrasting colors to form a floor-to-ceiling panel behind the sink and mirror, this bathroom, which could have looked bland and boring if pale tiles had been used exclusively, now has extra warmth and visual appeal.

The inset tiles below the lights on the adjacent wall provide additional interest and keep the area from being dominated by the darker color.

Many marble tiles are fairly large, and this bathroom demonstrates the benefits of using large tiles rather than small ones when tiling entire walls, especially in a small room. Small tiles produce a surface that looks busier and actually emphasizes the small size of a room; large tiles have just the opposite effect.

► Although the strong color of these backsplash tiles contrasts nicely with the more neutral tiles used in the rest of the bathroom, the edges of the backsplash were given additional punch by adding patterned dado or border tiles.

Black and white

The stark contrast between black and white tiles is played up effectively in both bathrooms and kitchens, whether the black tiles are used for simple accents or more boldly to cover large areas. Instead of creating a dark or depressing look, large areas of black tiles suggest an air of luxury and style. They are especially effective when used in a high-tech bathroom with lots of chrome and stainless-steel fixtures and accessories.

◀ Tiling in black and white has long been a popular choice for bathrooms; the black tiles usually are used as accents to break up an overall white scheme. But larger areas of black tiles also make a dramatic statement, as in this small bathroom. Here, they form a backdrop for the toilet and line the low tub surround.

To add further interest, white tiles with simple black border patterns were used to make rectangular outlines on this white background. Needless to say, intricate patterns like this require careful planning. In fact, it's a good idea to sketch the actual layout to make sure you're happy with the final arrangement (see pages 30–31).

▶ Using tiles of one color for a backsplash, whether it's in a kitchen or bathroom, can be boring, especially if the tiles are white. However, you can add visual interest without adding color. This all-white backsplash is enlivened by dado tiles with a molded relief pattern. The shapes in the pattern are enhanced by the interplay of light and shadow, and they change with the lighting, adding a subtle accent to the backsplash.

◀ Specially made dado tiles often are a different size than the field tiles that surround them, so there's no point in trying to keep the joints aligned. Instead, deliberately stagger the joints so they don't align anywhere at all.

Combining standard tiles of different sizes can present problems, though. For example, this striking black-and-white backsplash is made up of 4-inch-square black tiles, but the dado running through the center uses 8-inch-square tiles with a printed checkerboard pattern.

Although these dado tiles are twice the width of the field tiles, they make no allowance for the grout joint between the two smaller tiles. Consequently, for all the joints to line up, you'd need to allow for wider joints between the large tiles or narrower joints between the smaller tiles (or a combination of the two). Again, careful layout is especially important; it's a good idea to use strips of cardboard or other suitable spacers to position the tiles.

Country style

The wide variety of tiles available makes it possible to match any decor imaginable—from simple country style to modern high-tech. No matter what the style of your room, you'll find tiles that will fit right in. For a country look, subdued tones are best, especially when teamed with old-fashioned bathroom fixtures and natural-finish wood cabinets. The tiles should make a pleasing but unobtrusive backdrop to the room's fixtures and accessories, lending a sense of harmony and softness.

◀ Half-tiling bathroom walls often is as effective as tiling them completely, and it also reduces the cost of the job. The tiles provide an easy-to-clean, water-resistant surface for the area of the walls that's most likely to be splashed from the sink or the tub.

The tiles should be installed to dado or waist height—or high enough above the sink to provide an effective backsplash. When laying them out, first plan the dado height, then mark off the wall down to the floor, starting with a whole tile at the top. Unless the floor is completely level, position the dado line to leave a partial tile at the bottom.

Although you can leave the edges of the top tiles showing—if they're glazed—it's much more attractive to add an actual dado, such as tiles or a wood molding.

◄ Backsplashes, whether they're in the kitchen or the bathroom, don't offer as many opportunities for laying out intricate designs as complete walls do. In such a small area, too busy a pattern or layout could look out of place. Still, a backsplash doesn't have to be restricted to one type and color of tile. With a little imagination, you can achieve an attractive arrangement.

Here, for example, a horizontal row of alternating blue and pale green tiles at countertop level is divided from the rest of the diagonally tiled beige backsplash by a half-round dado molding in blue and green. To add interest to the larger area of tiles behind the cooktop, a simple diamond motif was introduced, using two blue and two green tiles.

When a dado is incorporated in a kitchen backsplash this way, it's best to position it one tile above the countertop. In this location, it won't be hidden by the cupboards above and also won't interfere with electrical outlets on the wall.

◄ To add visual interest to this tiled backsplash without running a dado through it, the larger area of tiles behind the cooktop was treated to a simple diagonally tiled panel outlined by molded dado tiles. Notice that the joints of the dado tiles are longer than the field tiles and that they've been staggered in relation to them.

The ends of the dado tiles also have been mitered at the corners— something best done with a tile saw.

Bold colors

Many people prefer tiled surfaces that are subtle in appearance and that form a neutral backdrop for the other features in a room. On the other hand, using bold tile colors produces eye-catching effects that have dramatic impact. In these instances, the tiles become the major decorative element, so be sure to choose colors and patterns that will stand the test of time: Changing wallpaper and paint that you've grown tired of is relatively easy, but replacing tiles is a much more difficult and expensive job.

With bold color schemes, it's a good idea to draw up a plan on paper before you start to tile. When you've decided on the scheme you want, put the plan away for a week or so, then come back to it to see if it's one you still like. Once the tiles are on the wall, you'll have to live with them.

◄ Although it's usually much better to use large tiles when tiling a large area (especially entire walls), small mosaics also are effective. The individual mosaic pieces are so small that the eye doesn't immediately recognize them as individual pieces. Instead, and especially with a random combination of colors such as this, the wall takes on a pleasing mottled appearance. Glass mosaics such as these come in a wide variety of intense colors that would look out of place on a larger tile.

Another advantage of small mosaics is that they're ideal for tiling curved surfaces.

▶ A backsplash often can tolerate a pattern or color combination that would be too overwhelming on a larger scale. These two strong blues, for example, make a striking but simple statement, turning the backsplash into a strong visual element in the decor of this kitchen. The subtle color of the cabinets and countertop only reinforce this effect.

Be careful with this type of color scheme, though; if it's used with bold cabinet or countertop colors, it could result in visual chaos.

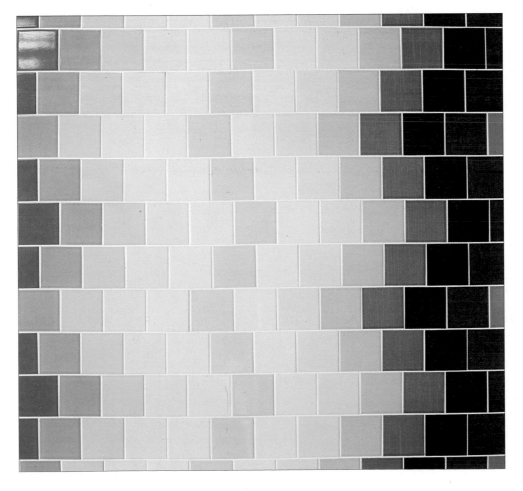

◀ Giving free rein to your imagination can produce stunning tile combos. Here, a variety of plain colors was combined to produce a dramatic graduated effect. Although not for everyone, this design makes a powerful statement in a bathroom.

Types of tile

No matter what you want to tile—whether it's a small backsplash behind a sink or a complete bathroom—your choice of tiles is positively huge. For the widest selection, go to a specialty tile outlet. They'll be able to help you determine how many tiles you'll need and also what other supplies and materials may be necessary. Tile sizes vary from small mosaics of about 1-inch square up to large marble and ceramic tiles that are 12 inches square or even 16 by 10 inches.

An important consideration is whether the tiles have glazed or unglazed edges. With the latter, unless you're tiling a wall from end to end and top to bottom or a backsplash that's bordered on all four sides, you'll need a way to conceal the edges around the perimeter of the tiled area. Fortunately, special border tiles are made just for this purpose. Or, you can use plastic tile trim or even a wooden molding to cover the edges.

STANDARD

These ceramic wall tiles offer you a wide range of colors, patterns, and sizes from which to choose. They're usually square, but you also can find oblong tiles that can be arranged in a bricklike pattern for extra interest. Smaller tiles are better for backsplashes than large ones. Some tiles are especially dense because they've been fired to higher temperatures than ordinary wall tiles. This creates a hard, glazed surface that's particularly good for kitchen countertops.

MOSAICS AND INSERTS

Mosaics are simply small tiles, often less than 2 inches square. They usually come in sheets on either a mesh backing or with a paper facing that holds the individual tiles together. Their small size makes them ideal for backsplashes. And, sheets of the smallest mosaics are especially easy to apply to curved wall surfaces.

Another type of small tile is the insert—a simple colored square that's designed to fit at the point where the corners of four tiles meet. They provide a simple way to break up a large expanse of plain tiles. Special tiles with one corner cut off accommodate the inserts.

HAND-PAINTED

BORDERS AND DADOES

Most patterned tiles feature printed designs, but you also can find hand-painted tiles with unique decorative motifs. They make wonderful insets, adding visual appeal to an otherwise plain area of tiles. No two hand-painted designs will be the same, which only adds to their appeal.

Occasionally, several tiles will be used together to form a larger picture or motif. You can position them like a conventional picture, possibly even outlining them with border or dado tiles.

From narrow pencil tiles—tiles that are a scant ½ inch wide—to wider picture tiles, borders and dadoes come in a variety of sizes, colors, patterns, and shapes. Although they're usually set in horizontal bands to break up or frame a large expanse of plain tiles, they also are used vertically. Or, use them to frame panels of tiles in contrasting colors or patterns. Tiles with molded relief patterns bring the added dimension of shape to a tile scheme.

MARBLE AND MOORISH

Genuine marble and simulated marble tiles let you create classically inspired tile schemes. Because genuine marble tiles are expensive, one way to achieve the same effect is to use simulated-marble field tiles for most of the work and genuine marble borders and dadoes as visual accents. For a more exotic appearance, you also can choose tiles inspired by the bold colors and patterns of Moorish designs.

INSETS AND FEATURES

You'll also find special tiles that can be used as visual accents in a tile scheme. For example, inset tiles come in standard sizes but have a central motif. They can be arranged in random or regular patterns among plain tiles. In some cases, two or more tiles will fit together to make a larger picture.

With their uneven shapes and quaint hand-painted designs, handmade tiles from countries such as Africa and Mexico provide even more interest to your tile schemes. Some feature faux crackling for an antique look.

Preparation

Before starting any wall tiling—whether it's a simple backsplash behind a sink or a complete bathroom—it's essential to make sure the surface you'll be tiling is sound and flat.

Tiles can be applied to a variety of wall surfaces: plaster, drywall, plywood, painted surfaces, and even old ceramic tiles. But to ensure good results, the surface must be dry, free of dust, and completely sound and stable.

If necessary, take the time to properly prepare the surface to make it smooth, strong, and uniform. In extreme cases, you may have to remove old plaster from a wall and either replaster it or put up new drywall. Don't rush this stage of the job; the time and effort you invest in surface preparation will pay dividends later.

Tools and materials

Even if you plan only to tile a small backsplash, you'll need a few special tiling tools to do the job right. Once you have the basics, you can add tools for specific jobs if and when you ever need them. You'll also need a few general-purpose tools, but they're probably ones you already own.

The materials you'll need for tiling will depend on your specific project. In some cases, besides the tiles, all you'll need is the appropriate adhesive and grout and some tile spacers.

PREPARATION

Screwdriver

Paintbrush

Hammers

Cold chisel
For chipping out damaged tiles and old adhesive

Filling knife
For removing wallpaper and loose paint and filling cracks and holes

Steel float
For filling large areas of damaged plaster

Sanding block
Silicone carbide paper
For giving surface of old tiles "tooth" for new tile adhesive
Sandpaper
For sanding down filler when preparing walls

TILING

Level

Tape measure

Small trowel
For scooping adhesive onto wall and grout onto tiles

Masking tape
Prevents drill bit from skidding off tile

Electric drill
For drilling tiles when removing them or attaching hardware

Small hacksaw
Cuts plastic corner trim and bath-sealing strip

Sealant dispenser
Use when applying silicone sealant

Crafts knife
Cuts mesh backing of mosaics

Notched adhesive spreader

Grout spreader (squeegee)

Grout shaper
Finishes grout joints neatly

Clean cloth

Sponge

Plastic scouring pad
Removes excess epoxy grout from countertop tiles

Tile scorer/grout raker
For scoring tiles when cutting or removing old grout

Toothed grout raker
Removes old grout from narrow joints

Tile-cutting tools

Tile spike
For scoring tiles when cutting

Combined cutting wheel/snapper
Scores and snaps tiles

Tile-cutting machine
Measures, scores, and cuts tiles

Nibblers
Removes narrow strips or waste from intricate shapes

Tile saw
Cuts intricate shapes or molded tiles

Tile file
For cleaning up edges of tiles after cutting

MATERIALS

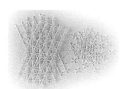

Bath trim
Makes a waterproof seal between the tub and wall when tiles are set over its vertical lip

Cross-shaped tile spacers
Ensures uniform joints between tiles

Plastic corner trim
For finishing external corners of walls and edges of backsplashes when using tiles with unglazed edges

PERSONAL PROTECTION

Thick gloves
Protect hands when chipping out tiles

Safety goggles
Protect eyes from flying fragments when chipping out tiles

ADHESIVE

Adhesive for adhering ceramic tiles to walls is available both premixed and in powdered form for mixing with water. Premixed adhesive is more convenient to use, but powder is less expensive and may be worth considering for a large job. Various sizes are available, and the coverage is specified on the container. There are two basic types of adhesive:

All-purpose

A water-resistant adhesive suitable for use in kitchens and bathrooms. Some all-purpose adhesives also can be used as grout, but make sure this use is specified on the container before you apply it this way.

Waterproof

Use in areas where the tiles will be regularly subjected to a lot of moisture, such as on the walls of a shower.

GROUT

Grout comes both powdered for mixing with water and premixed. A hardener must be added to epoxy grout before use. White grout is the most common, but other colors also are available. The container will specify the coverage you can expect. Various types are available:

Standard

Use where the tiles are unlikely to come into contact with water.

Water-resistant

For backsplashes and general kitchen and bathroom tiling.

Waterproof

Use where the tiles will be subjected regularly to moisture, such as on the walls of a shower.

Epoxy

A hard, waterproof grout that won't harbor germs; ideal for kitchen countertops.

Types of surfaces

In some cases, you may want to tile a wall that was previously painted or papered. You can apply tiles directly over gloss and water-based paints if the underlying plaster and the paint itself are sound. In that case, only minimal preparation will be needed before you tile. But if your walls have some other kind of painted finish, you may have to strip them completely; some painted finishes just don't make a stable base for tiling. Wash them off or remove them with the appropriate stripper, then seal the surface.

Old wallpaper should be stripped completely. Whether you use the traditional soak-and-scrape method that's shown below or a steam stripper, make sure the wall is completely dry before you start to tile.

TOOLS: Bucket, sponge, wallpaper scraper, sanding block, large paintbrush, hammer, cold chisel, small trowel, lath or furring strip

MATERIALS: Wallpaper stripper, sandpaper, all-purpose cleaner, sealer/tile-adhesive primer, premixed mortar/one-coat plaster, silicone carbide paper

PREPARING THE WALL

1 If the wall originally was papered, soak the paper with a solution of wallpaper stripper, and scrape off the paper. Vinyl coverings should be peeled off and their backing paper stripped to expose the plaster. Also remove any lining paper.

2 On painted surfaces, scrape off any flaking paint with coarse sandpaper until you have a sound surface. To help the tiles stick to the wall, tooth the paint by scoring it with a scraper. Wash the area with all-purpose cleaner to remove dust and grease.

3 Whatever the surface, it should be sealed with the appropriate commercial sealer or tile-adhesive primer. Dilute the product you're using and apply it according to the manufacturer's instructions. Allow it to dry completely.

OLD CERAMIC TILES

You can retile directly over existing ceramic tiles if the tiles are securely attached to the wall and give you a reasonably flat surface for the new tiles. If possible, arrange the new tiles so they overlap the joints of the old ones; this will give you a stronger tiled surface.

1 If any of the original tiles are broken, loose, or hollow-sounding, carefully rake out the surrounding grout using a nail, and chip out the tiles with a hammer and cold chisel. Dampen the wall behind them, and fill any gaps you find with mortar or plaster.

2 Make the mortar or plaster exactly level with the surrounding tiles by working a small piece of wooden lath or furring strip across the area using a gentle sawing motion. Fill any depressions with more mortar or plaster, then check again for level and let the surface dry.

3 Although the surface of existing ceramic tiles should provide a sound enough base for your new tiles, you can make doubly sure by rubbing the tiles with silicone carbide paper. This will scratch the glaze and give a nice tooth to the tile adhesive.

4 Finally, thoroughly wash the tiles with soapy water to remove all traces of dust and grease. Make sure they're completely dry before you start to apply new tiles.

Cracks and holes

You need a reasonably flat surface for applying tile. Although tile adhesive can ride out depressions in the wall that are up to about ¼ inch deep, any greater surface irregularities will be reflected in your finished tiled surface. It's a good idea to check the flatness of your wall with a long, wooden straightedge.

You can chisel out small bumps and fill any resulting depressions. Similarly, fill all low areas; if necessary, clean them out and deepen the depression before you fill it. If the wall is very uneven, you may need to apply a skim coat of fresh plaster or even put up new drywall.

You can tile over small cracks in plaster, but be sure to fill larger ones. Clean out loose areas of plaster, then fill or replaster the area before tiling.

TOOLS: Steel rule, hammer, filling knife, old paintbrush, small trowel, chisel, steel float, short furring strip or lath, sanding block

MATERIALS: Filler, one-coat plaster or premixed mortar, coarse sandpaper, masonry nails, sealer/tile-adhesive primer

1 Large cracks in plaster should be filled. First, work the corner of the filling-knife blade along the crack to undercut the edges (so the filler will have a good grip), then brush out all dust and loose debris. Use an old paintbrush to dampen the crack and press filler into it with the knife. Dampen the straight edge of the blade and use it to level the filler with the surrounding wall.

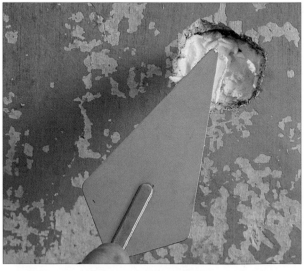

2 Filler won't dry properly if it's applied too thickly, so fill deep holes in two or more stages. Use a small trowel to insert the first layer, using the point to work the filler down into the crevices at the bottom of the hole.

3 When the first layer of filler is dry, add another layer with the filling knife, pressing it in firmly and striking it off level with the surrounding plaster.

4 Don't worry about minor damage to external corners; the tiles and/or corner trim will cover any slight gaps. However, where large portions of plaster are missing, build up the corner with the appropriate filler or one-coat plaster. Temporarily nail a furring strip to one edge to provide a support for the filler.

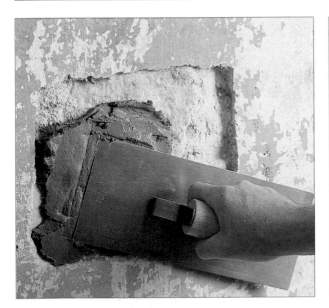

5 Make sure the plaster is in contact with the wall by rapping it with your knuckles; where it's come away from the underlying surface, you'll hear a hollow sound. Clean out these areas with a hammer and chisel, undercutting the edges. Then fill with one coat plaster or mortar, using a furring strip to level it with the surrounding plaster.

6 Allow any filled areas to dry completely, then sand them smooth with coarse sandpaper wrapped around a sanding block. You don't need the perfectly smooth surface you would for painting, but the filled area should be level with its surrounding surface. Finally, seal the wall with the appropriate sealer or tile-adhesive primer.

Boxing in and paneling

Wherever possible, pipes that run down or along walls should be concealed by boxing them in, then tiling the box as usual. You can make the box with drywall, medium-density fiberboard (MDF), or marine-grade plywood where damp conditions are a problem. The box needs to be rigid to avoid cracking the grout between the tiles, so use screws instead of nails to build it. If the box conceals a hot-water pipe, insulate the pipe; otherwise, heat may cause the wood to shrink, again causing cracked grout.

Be sure to seal all wood surfaces with a solvent-based primer before tiling.

TOOLS: Steel tape measure, pencil, saw, awl, electric drill, wood bit, masonry bit, countersink bit, screwdriver

MATERIALS: 1 x 2-inch or 1-inch battens, ½- or ¾-inch marine-grade plywood/MDF/drywall, screws, wall anchors

CONCEALING PIPES

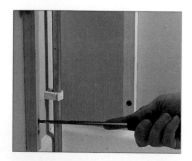

1 Where pipes run down a corner of the room, attach 1-inch-square vertical battens to each wall, securing them with countersunk screws driven into wall anchors. Position the battens so that the size of the finished box won't require any cut tiles.

2 Cut two sections of ¾-inch-thick marine-grade plywood or MDF to the right size, and butt-join them along their outside edges using countersunk screws. Then screw the assembled panels to the wooden battens that you've already attached to the wall.

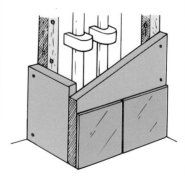

BOXING IN PIPES

You won't need a separate framework if you butt-join boards at the corner and screw them to wood strips.

PANELING A TUB

1 A freestanding bathtub can be made to look like a built-in if it's given a tiled tub surround.

The procedure is essentially the same as for boxing in pipes: A wooden framework is built around the tub and paneled to prepare it for tiling. Build a framework around the tub using 1×2-inch lumber screwed to the adjacent walls and floor for a rigid structure. If you have an acrylic or fiberglass tub with wooden reinforcements around the edge, screw the frame to it. Or, simply build the framework slightly lower than the top of the tub so you can support the lip and tile below it.

2 Panel the framework with ½-inch marine-grade plywood, attaching it with countersunk screws. Make sure the screw heads are below the surface; otherwise, they'll get in the way of the tiles and make the surface uneven.

3 At the faucet and drain end of the tub, make an access panel, or buy a ready-made double-lipped door or panel and attach it with magnetic catches. The panel must be large enough to allow access to all the plumbing. After tiling, conceal the edges of the panel with silicone sealant, which will let you remove the panel.

COVERING BARE BRICK WALLS

To tile a bare brick wall, you first must cover it with plaster, drywall, ½-inch plywood, or sheets of MDF.

First, attach the framework to the wall using 1×2-inch vertical furring strips spaced no further than 12 inches apart. In addition, run horizontal furring strips along the top and bottom of the wall. Frame window and door openings completely.

Screw the furring strips to the wall using a long straightedge and a level to make sure they're all in line from top to bottom, as well as vertically. If necessary, shim them with scraps of wood. Then attach the panels using countersunk screws.

When using plywood as a base for tiling, choose waterproof plywood in case moisture seeps through any of the joints. This is doubly important when framing a shower stall.

Planning and Laying Out

Careful planning and layout are critical to the success of any tiling project. You need to decide on the type and size of tiles you want, determine how many to buy, work out how to arrange them on the wall so they look their best, and determine where on the wall to begin setting them to achieve a pleasing symmetrical appearance.

Because there are so many tile designs to choose from and so many ways to use them, you need to have a clear idea of your layout and your plan before you start. The best way is to sketch your plan on paper. In fact, a paper plan is almost essential for correctly determining how many tiles to buy. You also can use your sketch to determine where to put dadoes, borders, inset tiles, and picture panels.

When you know what to use and how, you can start work on the wall itself by marking the horizontal and vertical starting lines and nailing battens to the wall to support the tiles.

This chapter contains

Planning

When you've decided on the types of tiles you want to use, you need to determine just how many you'll need. The first step is to calculate the area to be tiled, whether it's a simple backsplash or a complete room. The easiest way to do this is to draw up a plan, mark all the relevant dimensions on it, and calculate the surface area. Tiles are sold in packs, boxes, and cartons that come in various sizes; your supplier can help you figure out how many tiles you'll need.

Remember to allow extra for cutting in around edges and for breakage. For an area of 5 square yards, buy 10 percent more than you need; for a larger area, add an extra 5 percent. Work out the tiling pattern and determine where you'll place inset tiles and whether you'll want a dado or border tiles. With dado and border tiles, you'll need to know the total length instead of the surface area.

DRAWING A PAPER PLAN

Draw a plan of the wall, or portion of wall, to be tiled. If you're tiling a whole room, draw each wall separately. There's no need to make your drawings accurate in terms of scale; simply use them as a visual guide to the important features you need to include in your calculations. However, the dimensions you mark on your plan should be taken from accurate measurements. Use these dimensions to calculate the actual area you'll need to tile. If you're unsure how to do this, take the plan to your tile supplier, who will be able to make the calculations for you.

For a whole room, draw up a plan like this, marking on it the dimensions of the walls, windows, doors, and other features.

For each feature, multiply the length by the height to calculate its area, then add all of your figures together. Subtract your result from the total wall area to get the area that needs tiling.

Use this figure to determine the number of tiles you'll need to buy, as well as quantities of supplies like adhesive and grout.

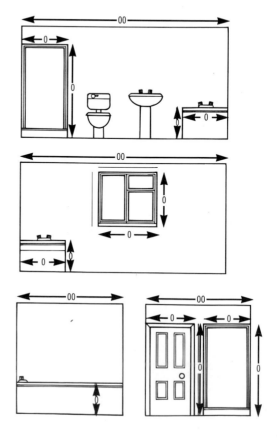

TILING PATTERNS

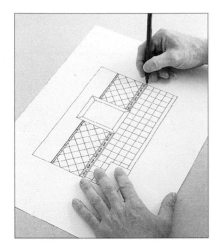

Although tiles usually are lined up both horizontally and vertically, they also can be arranged in diagonal rows or in a brick pattern to provide additional interest. You can create especially attractive designs by combining these arrangements in bands separated by patterned or contrasting dado tiles.

To work out the most attractive pattern, use a large sheet of paper to draw up another plan of the walls—one that will give you plenty of room to fill in all the details. After drawing in the relevant features, add the positions of patterned tiles, insets, dadoes, etc. Or use your plan to decide on the kind of tile layout you want. Photocopy your original drawings of the walls, and sketch several layouts to see which one you like best.

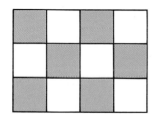

The conventional method of arranging tiles is to align the rows both horizontally and vertically, creating continuous horizontal and vertical joints.

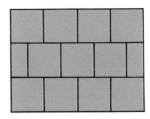

For added interest, you can stagger the tiles in each row relative to the adjacent rows in brick fashion. This works well with rectangular tiles.

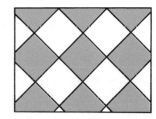

You can achieve another attractive pattern by setting the rows of tiles diagonally to create a diamond pattern. This works best with square tiles.

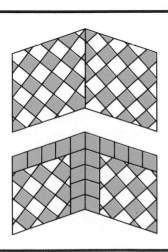

COPING WITH CORNERS

If you plan to arrange the tiles in a particular pattern or are using patterned tiles and are tiling adjacent walls, continuing the pattern from one wall to another can be quite difficult (top)—especially if the corners of the room aren't perfectly vertical. In fact, in some situations, it may not be possible to do at all.

A simple solution to the problem is to edge the patterned area of tiles with plain tiles set in conventional vertical and horizontal rows. This has the effect of creating patterned panels (bottom).

Laying out

After buying your tiles and preparing the wall for tiling, you can begin your layout. This step is essential for determining where to set the first tile and for making sure that the layout will be symmetrical.

   You'll need to support the tiles while the adhesive dries; otherwise they'll slide down the wall. To do this, temporarily nail a horizontal strip of wood near the base of the wall. You can't rely on the baseboard or floor for support because neither is likely to be perfectly level.

TOOLS: Tape measure, pencil, level, long straight-edged furring strip, gauge rod, hammer

MATERIALS: Two 1×2-inch straight pine furring strips, masonry nails

MAKING A GAUGE ROD

1 To make a gauge rod, lay out a row of tiles with tile spacers between them. Place the wood strip alongside so one end is level with the edge of the first tile. Mark the tile positions on it, allowing for the gaps in between. With handmade tiles, which are irregular in size, allow a spacing of (³⁄₁₆–⁵⁄₁₆ inch).

A gauge rod is a handy tool for tiling a large area, and it's easy to make from a wooden furring strip about 6 feet long (or shorter if you're tiling a short wall). It lets you determine where the horizontal and vertical rows of tiles will fall on the wall so you easily can see whether tiles need to be cut at the ends of the rows and, if so, by how much. Using the rod, you also can determine the positions of the supporting wooden furring strips.

2 For easy reading, extend the pencil marks across the entire face of the rod, making sure they're square to the edge. You can do this using another tile as a guide. If you like, you can number the divisions on the rod so you can see at a glance how many tiles there will be in each row.

LAYING OUT

1 Measure the length of the wall and make a pencil mark at the center. Then, holding the straight-edged wood strip vertically, use a level to draw a vertical line from the floor to the ceiling at the point of the mark.

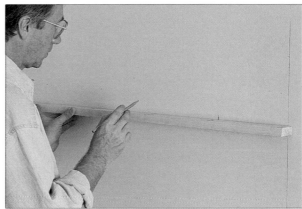

2 Hold the mark at the end of the gauge rod against the line on the wall to determine where the vertical rows of tiles will fall. On a long run, it may help to mark off the tile positions on the wall.

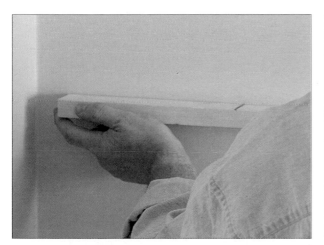

3 At the end of the wall, the gauge rod will show whether you need a cut tile and, if so, how wide it should be. Because you began from the center of the wall, you'll also need the same width of tile at the other end of the wall. If you're left with an extra-narrow gap to fill, it may be hard to cut a narrow enough sliver. And if the corner is uneven, you may run into serious problems when the sliver tapers to practically nothing.

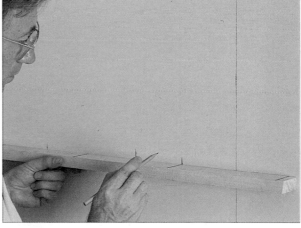

4 Your finished tiled wall will look best if any cut tiles are at least half a tile wide. So go back to your center line, and hold the gauge rod so its end mark is offset to one side of the center line by half a tile width. Then make a mark on the wall in line with the end mark. Draw a new vertical line at this point, which now will be your starting point. This way, the actual center line of the wall will pass through the center of a tile.

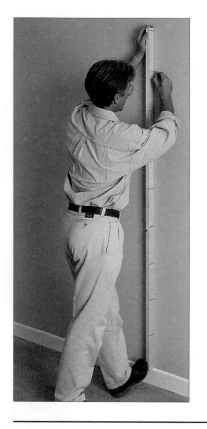

5 Next, determine the positions of the horizontal rows of tiles. First, hold the gauge rod against your vertical starting line with one end touching the wall's baseboard or floor. Then make a pencil mark on the wall so that it's level with the topmost mark on the gauge rod.

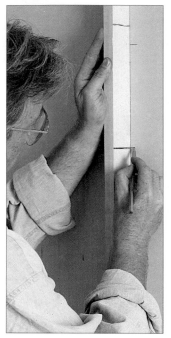

6 Hold the end of the rod against the ceiling and check to see if any mark on it aligns with the wall mark. If it does, you won't need to cut tiles for the top and bottom rows. If it doesn't, look at the gap between the wall mark and the nearest mark on the rod below it; halving this distance gives the depth of the cut tiles at top and bottom. If they're very narrow, mark the wall level with the next mark down on the rod. Ceilings are rarely level and often will require you to cut tiles.

7 Measure the distance between the two pencil marks on the wall. Then make a third pencil mark exactly midway between these two points. This will give you an idea of how deep to cut the tiles at the top and bottom.

8 Holding the gauge rod so one end is just above the baseboard and one of its marks is aligned with the third wall mark, make another mark on the wall at the foot of the rod. This will be your starting point for the first horizontal row of tiles and will help make sure that the cut tiles at top and bottom will be the same depth.

COPING WITH OBSTRUCTIONS

Windows, doors, and other fixtures complicate laying out a wall for tiling, especially if they're at one end of the wall. The important thing to remember is to work from the center of the most prominent visual feature when planning your layout. Be prepared to change your starting point if you run into problems with narrow cut tiles at the ends of the walls or at windows or doors. Take your time, and use the gauge rod to help determine the best starting point.

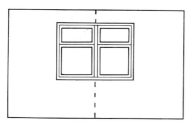

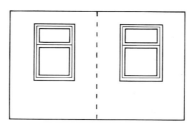

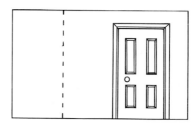

Where the wall includes a single window near its center, use the center line of the window as your starting point to lay out tiles with the gauge rod.

On a wall with two windows, it's best to work from the center line of the wall section between the windows; this will give your tiling layout a much more balanced and symmetrical look.

If the window or door is at one end of the wall, work from the center line of the wall section between the farthest corner and the door (or window frame) for a balanced look.

9 Nail a horizontal wooden furring strip to the wall in line with the pencil mark, using a level to make sure it's perfectly level. Don't drive the nails all the way in; leave their heads protruding so you can easily remove the strip.

10 When you start tiling, work out from the vertical starting line. Although you can align the tiles with this line, it will be easier if you have an exact edge from which to work. Nail a vertical wood strip to the wall along the pencil line.

Tiling a Wall

Tiling a large area such as a complete wall is an ambitious undertaking. But if you take your time and you've prepared the surface correctly, your results are bound to be good.

Although you need to work quickly, especially when applying grout, don't rush the job; you may make a mistake that you can't correct. Round up your tiles, adhesive, and tools as well as your paper plan so you'll be sure to place any patterned or inset tiles exactly where they belong. Tile a small area at a time, making sure the tiles are spaced evenly and bedded properly so they're all level.

A tile that's lower or higher than its surrounding tiles will ruin the appearance of your wall. Fix these problems while you're setting the tiles, not later when the adhesive has set.

Field tiles

When tiling a large area, begin by filling in the center portion with whole tiles, working out from the center and up from the bottom. These tiles are called field tiles. They're set in a bed of adhesive that's spread on the wall with a notched spreader that leaves ridges of adhesive rather than a smooth continuous layer.

To ensure uniform spacing between tiles, you can place plastic cross-shaped spacers between them or simply use pieces of cardboard or matchsticks. Work on a small area at a time; otherwise you may find that the adhesive starts to harden before you're finished.

TOOLS: Small trowel, notched adhesive spreader, sponge, bucket

MATERIALS: Tiles, tile adhesive, tile spacers, water

1 Because tile adhesive begins to harden once it's exposed to air, it's best to work on an area no greater than 1 square yard at a time. Use a small trowel to scoop some adhesive onto the wall, then spread it out horizontally with the notched spreader. Make sure that the teeth of the spreader actually touch the wall's surface so you're left with a series of parallel ridges of adhesive, as shown. Work away from the vertical guide batten.

2 Position the first tile so it sits on the horizontal batten and rests against the vertical batten. Press it firmly against the wall.

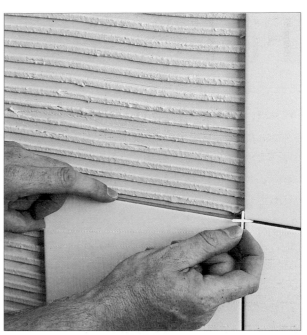

3 Add the next horizontal tile and the first tile in the row above, bedding them firmly in the adhesive by wiggling them slightly while pressing firmly with your hand. For now, space them by eye.

4 Add tile spacers to ensure even gaps. The adhesive is flexible enough to let you move the tiles slightly. Handmade tiles need larger gaps, so use cardboard or wood scraps as spacers.

5 Continue until you've tiled the entire area of adhesive. Then wipe the faces of the tiles with a damp sponge to remove any excess adhesive. This is essential; if you wait until the job is done, the adhesive will have hardened and will be more difficult to remove. Continue until all of the field tiles have been set on the wall.

MIXING TILES

Colored tiles or tiles with colored patterns may vary slightly in shade from batch to batch. Using tiles from one box at a time might result in definite color changes across the surface. These shading variations will be much less noticeable if you mix tiles from different boxes before you start work.

Fixing uneven tiles

When tiling a wall, your goal is to produce a perfectly flat surface. If you've prepared the wall properly, this shouldn't be too difficult. Handle any slight undulations in the wall surface by varying the thickness of adhesive.

   If you don't try to level the faces of the tiles, you risk ruining the appearance of your finished job: Any light that falls on the tiles will immediately spotlight the high and low areas by casting telltale shadows. So check often for low or high tiles, and if you find them, remove them and bed them in fresh adhesive so they're level with surrounding tiles.

TOOLS: Level, filling knife, notched adhesive spreader, claw hammer

MATERIALS: Tile adhesive

1 As you set tiles on the wall, check often that they're level by holding a level across them. It will clearly identify any tiles that are lower or higher than the ones that surround them.

2 If you find a tile that's too low or too high, carefully pry it from the wall using a flat-bladed tool, such as a putty knife. Be careful not to disturb or damage any of the surrounding tiles.

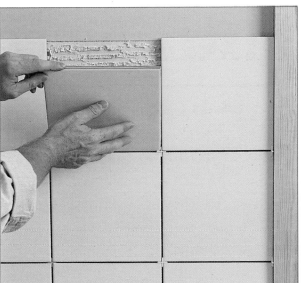

3 Scrape off the adhesive from the back of the tile and spread on a fresh layer using the notched spreader. If the tile was low, add a little more adhesive than normal; if high, a little less.

4 Press the tile back onto the wall, bedding it firmly and replacing any spacers in the grouting gaps. Make a final check with the level to ensure the tile is level.

REMOVING THE WOOD

1 Once you've tiled from the vertical wood strip to one end of the wall, you can remove the wood and work in the other direction. Then, when you've completed the wall above the horizontal furring strip, let the adhesive set before removing it. Use a claw hammer to pry out the nails so you can remove the strips of wood. Be careful not to disturb any tiles that butt up against them. Finally, fill in between the lowest row of tiles and the baseboard or the floor.

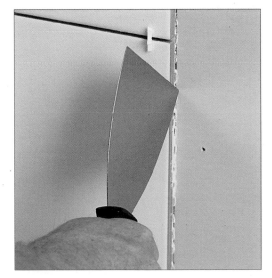

2 Use a filling knife to scrape away any adhesive that may have oozed out between the tiles and wood; it could prevent you from getting the correct spacing between the remaining tiles.

Inserting edge tiles

Unless you're extremely lucky and have a wall that's an exact number of whole tiles long and an exact number of whole tiles high, you'll need to cut some tiles to fill gaps at the ends and at the top and bottom. This isn't as difficult as it might at first seem, and, if they're used properly, the variety of cutting tools available will give you accurate cuts just about every time.

Accuracy is the key when cutting tiles. Take careful measurements of the spaces that need filling, and measure for each tile you need to cut: Don't assume that all the tiles needed to fill a gap along one end of a wall will be the same size. The corners of rooms rarely are truly square.

TOOLS: Tape measure, felt-tip pen, steel rule, glass cutter or tile spike, tile file, notched adhesive spreader

MATERIALS: Tiles, tile adhesive, tile spacers

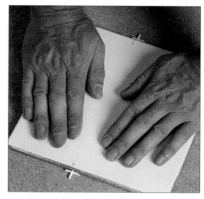

1 Take measurements at the top and bottom of the gap (or at each end if you're filling in at the ceiling or floor). If the tiled area will end at the adjacent wall, allow a gap for grouting; if the tiling will continue on that wall, the cut tile doesn't need to fit exactly into the corner; the tile on the adjacent wall will hide gaps.

2 Transfer the measurements to a tile with a felt-tip pen, remembering that the cut edge is the one that should fit into the corner. Then use a steel rule and a glass cutter or tile spike to score the glaze between the two marks. Press firmly and score the tile once only, with one smooth continuous movement.

3 Place the tile on a firm surface with one leg of a tile spacer under each end of the scored line. Then press down firmly on both sides of the line and the tile will snap cleanly in two. If it doesn't, you probably haven't scored the tile well enough, or the tile spacers may be out of line.

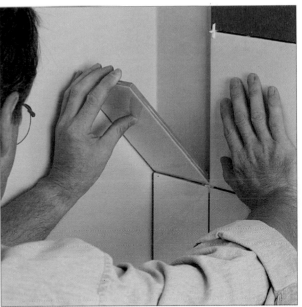

4 After cutting, clean up any rough edges of the tile with a tile file, holding it at a right angle to the edge.

5 Place the cut piece of tile in the gap to check for a tight fit. If necessary, make any adjustments with the tile file.

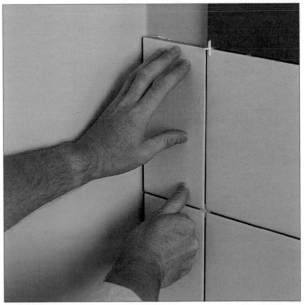

6 When you're happy with the fit, spread a layer of adhesive on the back of the cut tile, using the end of the notched spreader.

7 Press the tile firmly in place, wiggling it slightly to bed it and adjusting it so you can insert spacers at the top and bottom.

Methods of cutting

A glass cutter or tile spike is the simplest and least expensive tool for cutting tiles (see page 42), and for a small job it's probably not worth investing in anything else. Still, there are several more expensive tools that make the job of cutting tiles much easier. If you plan to cut a lot of tiles or if the tiles you're using are especially hard, it may be worth investing in one of them.

NIPPERS

If you only have a narrow sliver to remove from a tile or want to remove the waste from a cutout area of tile, nippers are a must. They let you grab a small portion of tile, then break it off by snapping down the tool.

To remove a narrow strip from the edge of a tile, score the glaze with a glass cutter. Then hold the tile firmly in one hand while gripping part of the waste close to the scored line with the jaws of the nippers. Snap down with the nippers and a piece of waste will break away along the scored line. Remove the rest of the waste in the same way.

COMBINATION CUTTING WHEEL/SNAPPER

This simple hand tool combines a cutting wheel for scoring the glaze of a tile with a pair of angled jaws that are used to snap it along the scored line. It's ideal for cutting small tiles or tiles with heavily studded backs.

1 Measure the gap to be filled and mark the tile as usual. Then, using a steel rule as a guide, run the wheel over the tile between the two marks to score it. Push down firmly and score the tile only once.

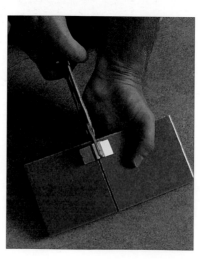

2 Place the tile in the jaws of the tool, aligning the scored line carefully with the center of the angled jaws. Squeeze the handles together and the tile will snap cleanly along the scored line; very little pressure is required. Be careful not to let the pieces drop; they may shatter if they fall and hit a hard surface.

TILE CUTTER

If you plan to cut a lot of tiles, especially if they're large and/or very hard, you'll probably want to invest in a tile cutter. At the very least, you'll want to rent one from a rental center. Several different models of tile cutters are available, some of which offer more features than others. All of them, however, are able to score tiles then cleanly snap them with very little pressure on your part.

1 Some tile cutters come with a removable gauge that lets you measure the gap to be filled. This particular model even makes an allowance for the grouting space and can be adjusted to measure a gap that tapers along its length. Position it so that the end of the gauge rests firmly against the adjacent wall or tiled surface and the tabs of the sliding portion rest against the edge of the adjacent tile. A simple lever then locks the gauge in this position, letting you transfer it to the tile cutter machine.

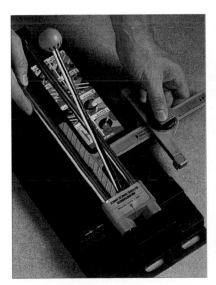

2 After locking the sliding portion of the gauge in place, fit the assembly into its cutout in the base of the tile cutter. Be careful not to disturb the gauge setting while you're doing this; otherwise you're liable to cut the tile to the wrong size.

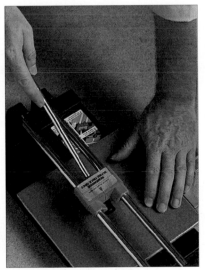

3 Place the tile in the machine, aligning one edge with the tabs of the gauge and the other with the stops molded into the base. Bring the scribe into contact with the tile, press down firmly, and push the handle forward to score the glaze.

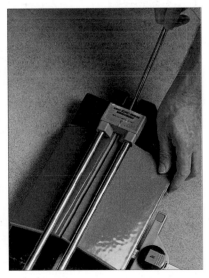

4 Set the tile under the handle slide so the scored line on the tile is aligned with the mark on the slide. Then lower the handle to bring the snapper into contact with the underside of the tile. Press down and the tile will snap in two.

Grouting

Once you've set all your tiles on the wall, let the adhesive dry before you grout the gaps between the tiles. The amount of time it will take for the adhesive to dry will vary with the type of adhesive you're using: Always refer to the manufacturer's instructions.

Some grouts come in powdered form for mixing with water, and others come premixed. Make sure you have enough to complete the tiled area, and be ready to work quickly; grout begins to harden right away and soon becomes unworkable. Make sure you use waterproof grout for a shower stall. Before applying the grout, remove the cross-shaped tile spacers or push them in as far as they'll go.

TOOLS: Small trowel, grout spreader/squeegee, grout shaper, sponge, bucket, soft clean cloth

MATERIALS: Grout, water

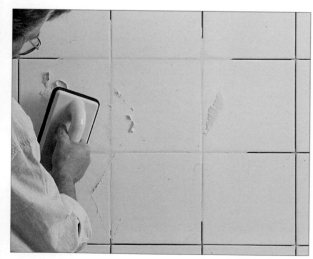

1 Use the trowel to scoop up some grout and press it onto the faces of the tiles. Then spread the grout with the squeegee, wiping it from the faces of the tiles and pressing it into the open joints. Use a smooth, diagonal, sweeping motion, working up and across the tiles. Work quickly until you've grouted all the joints.

2 Carefully go over the tiled area with a damp sponge to remove all traces of grout from the surfaces of the tiles. Do this as soon as you finish applying the grout; it will be much harder to remove after it hardens. Be especially careful not to drag the grout from the tile joints while you're doing this.

GROUT SHAPERS

You can buy a special tool for shaping grout or make your own. Some commercial grout shapers give you a choice of profile size and have interchangeable heads so that, when one becomes worn, you simply replace it.

Or, you can use a large-diameter wooden dowel, with the end neatly and smoothly rounded off, or even the tip of an old plastic paintbrush handle. If you choose either of these improvised tools, experiment on a small area of tiles first in case the material the tool is made of happens to discolor the grout.

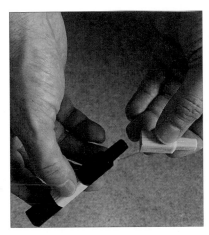

1 This commercial grout shaper features four interchangeable sections that give you a choice of shaping profiles. They also let you change to a fresh tip when the one you've been using becomes too worn.

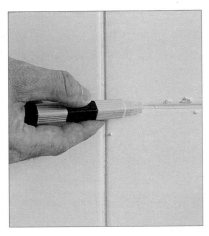

2 Shape the grout after it hardens slightly, holding the tool so it runs along the edges of the adjacent tiles with the corner of the tip smoothing the grout. Sponge off any grout that squeezes out at the sides.

3 Allow the grout to harden slightly, then shape the joints for a uniform appearance. Pull the shaper along each vertical and horizontal joint in one continuous movement. Remove any excess grout with a sponge.

4 If the shaping process exposes any gaps or holes in the grouted joints, press a small amount of fresh grout into them with your fingertip. Then shape the joint as before and remove any excess.

5 Let the grout harden completely. As the sponged faces of the tiles dry, you'll notice a powdery residue covering the surface. Wipe off this residue with a soft, clean cloth for a nicely polished finish.

Borders and Dadoes

Although there are many wonderful patterned tiles to choose from, many people feel that using them to tile an entire wall produces a look that's just too busy for their taste. Even if you only want to tile a small backsplash, you may prefer plain tiles. Still, a small area of plain tiles risks looking bland, and a large area, downright cold and uninteresting. Adding some form of pattern or contrasting color gives you a focal point and much-needed visual interest without becoming overwhelming.

The easiest way to do this is to add a border of contrasting tiles to backsplashes and half-tiled walls, or a dado course to a fully tiled wall. Although special narrow border and dado tiles are made just for this purpose, you also can use contrasting colored or patterned standard tiles this same way.

Another advantage of using dado tiles is that they give you a break between different colored or patterned tiles, or between different tile patterns on the same wall.

Border tiles

If you're tiling a small wall area such as a backsplash, or if you're half-tiling a wall, you may want to finish the edges with a contrasting or decorative border. You may have no choice if the tiles you're using don't have glazed edges. The simplest way to do this is to use standard tiles in a contrasting color or tiles with a pattern. Or, you may decide to use trim tiles or wooden molding.

On a sink backsplash, normal-size tiles may be too large, dominating the center part of the tiled area. In this case, it would be better to use a commercial border tile. They're much narrower than standard tiles and come in a variety of colors and patterns. Although you may be able to find border tiles that match the size of your field tiles, you probably won't, in which case you'll just have to stagger their joints relative to those in your field tiles.

TOOLS: Tape measure, felt-tip pen, steel rule, glass cutter or tile spike, tile file, small trowel, notched adhesive spreader, sponge, bucket

MATERIALS: Standard or border tiles, tile adhesive, tile spacers, water

STANDARD-SIZE TILES

The simplest way to add a border to a backsplash or similar small area of tiles is to use tiles of the same size as your field tiles but in a contrasting color or pattern. This is quite effective, but be careful not to let the border overpower the scheme, which it could easily do on such a small area.

When half-tiling a wall, you should make sure that the top row of tiles are whole tiles, not cut tiles. This will look better, whether or not you're using a contrasting border.

CHANGING DIRECTION

When setting border tiles around a backsplash, you may find you need to change the direction of the tiles from horizontal to vertical. If the tiles are a plain color, there won't be a problem; you can simply overlap the end of one tile with another. But if they're patterned tiles, this method won't give you a nice, neat corner because the pattern won't match. Don't worry. Fortunately, there are two possible solutions to the problem.

1 Depending on the pattern, it may be possible to miter the ends of the adjacent tiles so the design continues from the horizontal row onto the vertical row without an apparent break. You may need to trim the tiles to get a good match. Cut both before setting them on the wall.

2 After the tiles have been grouted, the mitered joint will look neat and unobtrusive. Note how the joints of the border tiles were staggered in relation to the joints of the field tiles. This was necessary because of their different sizes. This size variation between the two kinds of tiles is common.

3 In some cases, the pattern may be impossible to match up by mitering the ends of the border tiles. In this case, the answer is simply to fill the corner with a small square of plain tile, which you can easily cut from a larger tile.

4 Here, the square of tile was cut from one of the colored field tiles, but a plain white tile would have worked just as well. Make sure you use a tile with glazed edges and that you cut the square from a corner to give you two glazed sides.

Dadoes

A dado is a handy way to break up a large expanse of tiles, such as an entire wall. It encircles the wall at waist height and makes an ideal division between different colored or patterned tiles or between different tiling patterns, or it simply adds interest to an otherwise plain wall.

As with borders, you can use contrasting or patterned standard tiles to form a simple dado, which will unify your layout. Or, you could use a wooden dado rail or chair rail. Still, specially-made dado tiles will give you the greatest flexibility in terms of width, color, and pattern. In addition, many have a molded relief pattern that gives your tile design even more personality.

TOOLS: Tape measure, felt-tip pen, tile saw, small trowel, notched adhesive spreader, sponge, bucket

MATERIALS: Dado tiles, tile adhesive, tile spacers, water

CUTTING MOLDED TILES

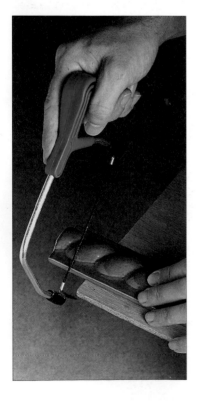

Dado tiles with a molded relief pattern are practically impossible to score and snap in the usual way when you have to cut them to length. The solution is to cut them with a tile saw. Simply mark the molded tile for length with a felt-tip pen, then cut along the line you've drawn with the tile saw.

CONCEALING THE END

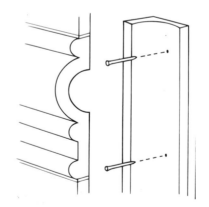

Dadoes don't have to be used solely to break up large expanses of standard tiles. They're just as effective when set into backsplashes, whether in the bathroom or the kitchen. Some, however, are formed into shapes that leave unsightly openings at the edges of a conventional backsplash. These openings need to be concealed, and the easiest way to do it is with decorative wooden molding.

Attach the molding to the edges of the backsplash with masonry nails. Using a nail set, drive the nails below the surface of the wood, fill the holes, and either stain or paint the molding.

◄ Here, a patterned dado tile makes an effective break between a lower panel of subtly colored tiles (which were set in a conventional pattern) from a panel of white tiles arranged diagonally. A small insert echoes the dado pattern and makes an effective accent on the stark white background.

▲ To break up an expanse of white tiles, this dado was created from three separate tiles. The central tile, with its olive-green relief pattern, is flanked by a narrow dado molding at the top and a pencil molding at the bottom, both in the same color.

◄ This diamond-patterned marble dado strip came on a mesh backing, much like mosaic tiles. Notice how a solid row of dark tiles was used above and below the dado course to further emphasize it.

Tiling Awkward Areas

When tiling a large area, such as a complete wall or even a complete room, you'll inevitably run into situations where you need to tile around corners or awkwardly shaped objects such as pipes, electrical outlets, and bathroom fixtures.

In some cases, where the obstruction is surface-mounted, it may be better just to remove it from the wall, set the tiles, then reattach the item, drilling any necessary holes through the tiles for the screws. This often will give you neater results than cutting individual tiles to fit around the obstruction. Still, that's just what you'll have to do if the object can't be taken down.

Tiling around corners is relatively straightforward, but cutting tiles to fit around odd shapes takes some time. It isn't especially difficult—just use the right technique and you'll get professional-looking results.

This chapter contains

Corners

The most common problem you'll face when tiling a wall is dealing with corners. You may have to tile around an external corner (one that projects out), an internal corner, or both. You'll use different techniques for each to get the neatest results. The most important thing to remember is that the horizontal rows of tiles on the adjacent wall have to align. Be especially careful when you lay out the job to make sure your support wood strips are perfectly aligned with each other; any misalignment is sure to stand out and will ruin the appearance of your walls. Make sure that external corners are truly vertical; check them with a level. If they're not, you'll need to slightly overlap the ends of the tiles, then add tile trim to finish the joint.

TOOLS: Tape measure, pencil, level, hacksaw, small trowel, notched adhesive spreader, sponge, bucket

MATERIALS: Tiles, tile adhesive, corner trim, tile spacers, water

INTERNAL CORNERS

At an internal corner, the tiles on one wall are set so they overlap the ends of the tiles on the adjacent wall. The result should be a neat grouted joint in the seam between the two walls.

You'll probably have to cut tiles to fit into the corner on both walls. But if possible, use whole tiles on one wall to conceal the cut edges of the tiles on the other wall.

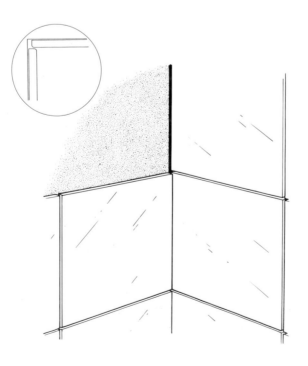

First tile one wall completely, cutting the edge tiles into the corner between the two walls. They don't have to be an exact fit since the overlapping tiles will hide any slight gap between them and the facing wall. When tiling the adjacent wall, be sure to take accurate measurements for each edge tile, allowing for the grout between it and the existing tiled wall. Then simply position the tiles to complete the corner.

EXTERNAL CORNERS

At an external corner, the simplest solution is to use plastic corner trim to hide the edges of the tiles and provide a neat finish for the joint between the adjacent walls. The trim has a quarter-round profile with a perforated mounting flange for embedding in the tile adhesive. They're available in a variety of colors and work for all thicknesses of tile.

1 Tile one of the walls completely so the edges of the tiles are flush with the end of the wall. Cut the corner trim to length with a hacksaw, then apply a narrow bead of tile adhesive to the face of the other wall (called the return wall) from top to bottom. Carefully press the trim into the adhesive, aligning it with the edges of the tiles on the adjacent wall. Remember to insert tile spacers between the trim and the edges of the tiles.

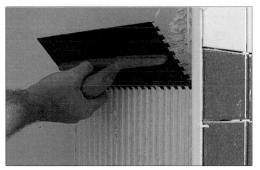

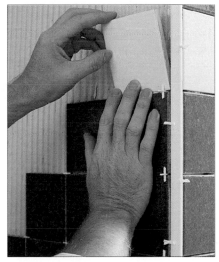

2 Spread more adhesive on the second (return) wall, moving the spreader vertically rather than horizontally. This will keep the spreader from catching the trim and pulling it away from the corner.

3 Tile the return wall, working away from the corner trim. Place the tiles so they almost touch the trim, then insert tile spacers between the trim and the tiles to ensure an even grouted joint. Grout the joints as usual when the adhesive is completely set.

GLAZED-EDGE TILES

If you're using tiles with beveled or rounded glazed edges, you can finish external corners without using corner trim, but only if the corner is truly vertical. Simply set the tiles on one wall so they overlap the edges of the tiles on the other wall.

Tile the return wall so the tiles are flush with the face of the main wall. Then simply set the glazed-edge tiles on the main wall so they overlap and conceal the edges of the tiles on the return wall.

Window recesses

Tiling a window recess has its own particular set of problems. In effect, it's a continuous external corner, which requires joining corner trim at the ends. In addition, the reveal area probably is narrow and will involve cutting tiles to fit the space. You'll also need to find a way to hold the tiles in place at the top of the recess until the adhesive has had a chance to set.

First, tile the face of the wall surrounding the window recess, then tile the underside of the reveal, the sides, and finally the bottom.

TOOLS: Tape measure, pencil, small trowel, notched adhesive spreader, glass cutter or tile spike, steel rule, hacksaw, hammer

MATERIALS: Tiles, tile adhesive, corner trim, wooden furring strips, masonry nails

1 Begin by tiling the face of the wall up to the window recess so the edges of the tiles are flush with the reveal. Cut lengths of corner trim to fit around the recess, mitering the ends so they fit neatly together.

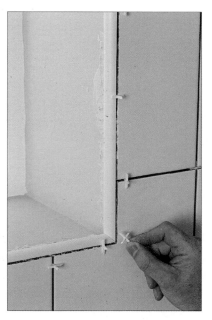

2 If you don't have a miter box, measure back along one side of the trim a distance equal to its width. Join this point with the opposite corner and saw off the triangular piece of waste. Insert spacers next to the trim.

3 To tile the reveal itself, set whole tiles around the outer edge of the reveal so that they butt up against the corner trim. Then fill in the remaining space against the window frame with cut tiles.

SUPPORTING THE TILES

The main problem with completely tiling a window recess is holding the tiles in place at the top of the recess while the adhesive sets. This applies to both the tiles on the face of the wall and on the underside of the reveal. The simplest solution is to use strips of lumber as temporary supports while the adhesive sets.

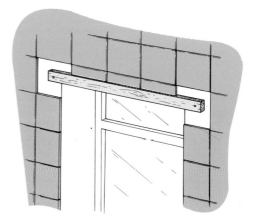

▲ To support the tiles on the face of the wall, temporarily nail a strip of wood in place so its upper edge is level with the underside of the reveal. When the tiles have been set in place and the adhesive is completely set, remove the wood and finish tiling the face of the wall where the batten was positioned.

◄ To support the tiles on the underside of the reveal while the adhesive sets, use a wooden furring strip wedged in place with two uprights.

OVERLAPPING EDGES

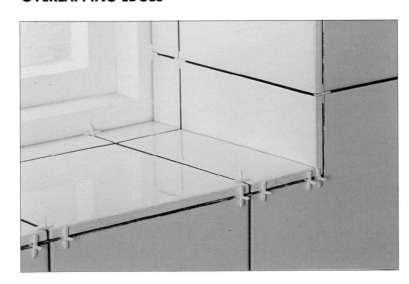

Tiles with glazed edges also can be used to finish a window recess, and you won't need the corner trim you'd normally have to use with external corners. One set of tiles—those on the horizontal windowsill—simply overlaps the edges of those on the adjacent vertical surfaces.

As with corner trim, set the tiles on the face of the wall so their top edges are flush with the reveal. Then set whole tiles in place around the recess so they overlap the edges of the tiles on the face of the wall.

Pipes

Some rooms you want to tile may have pipes that either pass through the wall or run along its face. Ideally, you should box them in to conceal them. But if boxing them in just isn't possible, you may have to cut a tile to fit around a pipe or drill the face of the tiles for pipe clips. Neither job is especially difficult—just remember to measure and mark carefully whenever you cut tiles to fit around a pipe.

You can use the same technique for tiling around an electrical outlet or switch. Here, however, don't begin work until you've turned off power for the circuit you're working on at the breaker box. Then remove the outlet or switch cover and tile up to the edges of the box behind it.

TOOLS: Pencil, felt-tip pen, steel rule, glass cutter or tile spike, narrow nippers, tile file, hammer, electric drill, masonry/tile bit, screwdriver

MATERIALS: Tiles, tile adhesive, pipe section, masking tape, masonry nail, wall anchors, screws, pipe clips

CUTTING AROUND A PIPE

If only one tile will be affected by the pipe, the best way to handle it is simply to split the tile on the center line of the pipe, and make a semicircular cutout in each half to fit around the pipe. If the pipe happens to fall on the joint between two tiles, just adapt this technique to cut away parts of both tiles.

2 Next, use a felt-tip pen to transfer the pencil marks to the tile you'll cut. An important point: Remember to insert tile spacers before transferring the marks to the tile so they'll be in the final, correct position.

1 After tiling the wall on one side of and below the pipe, use a tile and a pencil to mark lines on the wall level with the top, bottom, and sides of the pipe where it comes out of the wall.

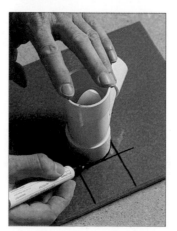

3 Using another tile as a guide to ensure that the lines are at a right angle to the edges of the tile, extend the marks across the face with your felt-tip pen. Where the pairs of lines intersect, carefully draw an outline around a cut-off section of pipe of the correct diameter to mark the area to be removed.

PIPE CLIPS

If you want to
run a pipe across
the face of a tiled
surface, you'll
have to drill holes
in the tiles for
attachment
screws, then
install pipe clips.
Use the same
technique for
attaching any
surface-mounted
fixture to a tiled
surface—a mirror,
toilet paper holder,
or soap dish.

1 Use masking tape to cover the area of the
tile to be drilled. This will let you mark the
hole positions with a pencil and help prevent
the drill bit from skidding—especially if you're
using a masonry bit. You can give your bit an
even better start by using a masonry nail to
break the glaze at each point to be drilled. A
light tap on the nail with a hammer is all that's
necessary. Then drill holes for the screws using a
bit that matches the size of the wall anchors
you're using.

2 After drilling the holes to the right depth,
remove the masking tape from the face of
the tile and insert plastic wall anchors in the
holes. Finally, attach the pipe and the pipe clip,
securing the clip to the wall by driving screws
into the plastic wall anchors.

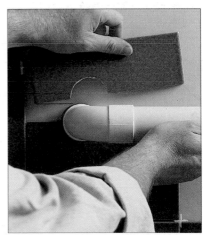

4 Score across the face of the
tile so the scored line passes
through the center of the circle.
Whether you score the line
vertically or horizontally will
depend on the way the pipe runs;
use the pipe itself to conceal as
much of the cut as possible. Then
snap the tile in two.

5 Using narrow nippers,
carefully remove the waste
from each semicircle. When you
get close to the line, position the
tile to check its fit. After you've
removed enough waste, carefully
smooth the edges with a tile file.
Then clean the face of the tile to
remove your pen marks.

6 Make a final check before
setting the pieces of tile on
the wall. Then apply adhesive
and stick them in place. If you
scored the tile correctly, the joint
between the two pieces should be
almost invisible. Fill any slight
gaps around the pipe when you
grout the tiles.

Bathroom fixtures

There may be times when you need to tile around a large, irregularly shaped object, such as a pedestal sink or other bathroom fixture. In these situations, the best solution is to pull the object away from the wall as far as possible, then tile the area behind it, even if this involves slight modifications to the plumbing. The neat job you'll do will more than make up for the extra work. But if this isn't possible, you'll need to make cutouts in the tiles that surround the fixture so they'll fit neatly against it.

TOOLS: Scissors, felt-tip pen, glass cutter or tile spike, steel rule, nippers, tile file, profile gauge, level, tape measure

MATERIALS: Tiles, paper, self-adhesive tape

IDEAL TOOLS

Tile saw

Although you can use nippers to make cutouts in tiles, you'll probably find a tile saw easier to use. A tile saw looks like a small hacksaw but has a special blade that will easily cut through ceramic tiles. After marking the tile area to be cut out, hold the tile firmly and simply saw along the outline. Because the blade is round, you can easily change direction to cut tight curves.

Profile gauge

A profile gauge is handy for transferring an unusual shape to a tile surface. It incorporates sliding plastic pins that conform to the  shape of an object when the tool is pushed against it. The gauge is best used for small tiles; for larger tiles, you'll probably have to find a way to hold the gauge in the right positions as you transfer the shapes to the larger surface area.

1 The simplest way to transfer the shape of a sink to the tile is to make a paper template. First, cut a piece of paper to the size of the tile, then make scissor cuts in the paper so you have a series of paper "fingers." The direction of these cuts will depend on the cutout's position. In this case, the shape will be in the corner of the tile so cuts go in both directions.

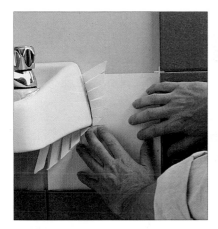

2 With tile spacers in place between the adjacent tiles, hold the paper in position as if it were a tile. Smooth the paper against the wall and fold the paper fingers back where they meet the sink.

3 Tape the fingers down to keep them from shifting, then lay the paper template on top of the tile to be cut. Carefully mark the outline of the template cutout on the tile surface with a felt-tip pen.

4 In this case, a large portion of waste is removed simply by scoring a line diagonally across it with a glass cutter or tile spike, then snapping it off with a pair of nippers. This will save you a lot of time.

5 The remaining waste must be removed with nippers. Don't try to snap off too much at once; take your time and break off small pieces, working toward the outline. As you get close to the line, take even smaller bites until you're scraping off slivers of tile.

6 Clean up the edges of the tile with a tile file, then hold the tile against the wall to check its fit around the sink. If necessary, further fine-tune the fit with the nippers and tile file. When you're satisfied that the gap around the sink is uniform, you can set the tile on the wall.

7 Continue to cut and fit tiles around the rest of the sink in the same way. When you're finished, you can tile the rest of the wall in the usual way. Finally, grout the gap between the tiles and the sink when you grout the rest of the tiles, and you'll have a nice, neat finish.

Backsplashes and Countertops

Tiles also can be used in smaller areas as stand-alone panels instead of major elements of the room. A backsplash behind a sink, around a tub, or along the back of a kitchen counter, for example, will protect the wall and provide an attractive decoration at the same time.

The techniques you'll use for tiling partial wall panels are essentially the same ones you used for tiling entire walls. Although the job of laying out the tiles is simpler, it's just as important. Pay special attention to waterproofing the joints between the tiles and a sink or tub.

Another small area that's perfect for tiling is a kitchen countertop, which can be tiled to match the backsplash behind it. You'll want to use special tiles and grout to make this important surface as durable and hygienic as possible.

Waterproof seals

When tiling a backsplash behind a sink or a bathtub, it's important to ensure a watertight seal along the bottom of the backsplash. This will prevent water from seeping through the joint and running down the wall behind it, which could happen even when waterproof grout is used.

In most cases, a bead of silicone sealant along the joint between the tiles and the sink or tub will be sufficient. An alternative is to use a plastic sealing strip, which is especially handy for bridging slight gaps between the bath and the tiled wall.

TOOLS: Sealant dispenser, hacksaw, tile saw

MATERIALS: Silicone sealant/plastic sealing strip/quarter-round tiles, tile adhesive, grout

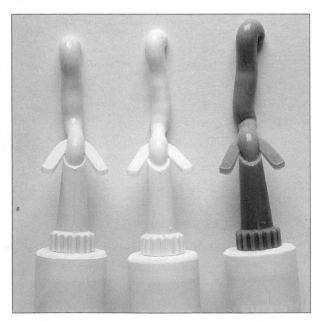

Silicone tile and tub sealants are available in white and a limited number of colors to match common bathroom fixtures. Some are sold in small squeeze-type dispensers that contain enough to run a bead around the average-size bathtub. Or, you can buy it in larger tubes for use with standard, trigger-type dispensers.

If you're using a trigger dispenser, place the nozzle of the sealant tube at one end of the backsplash and apply a smooth bead along its length, squeezing the trigger steadily as you go. You can smooth any slight irregularities with a finger moistened with water, but be careful; you could damage the appearance or, worse, the waterproof seal.

QUARTER-ROUND TILES

Although not as neat as plastic sealing strips, quarter-round tiles are handy for sealing a gap between a tiled backsplash and a tub. The narrow tiles have a curved profile that directs water back to the tub. They're available in a limited number of colors and sizes.

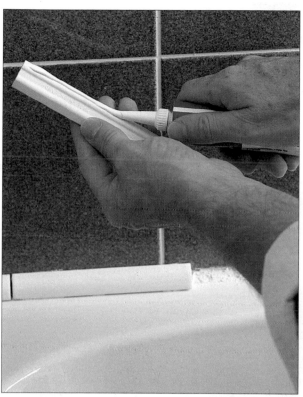

1 Each pack of quarter-round tiles should contain square-ended pieces, mitered pieces for corners, and bullnose stop-end pieces, together with the necessary adhesive.

2 Before setting the quarter-round tiles, it's a good idea to seal the gap between the tub and wall with silicone sealant. If you need to cut a tile, use a tile saw. Then set the tiles with adhesive.

3 Press the tiles firmly in place. Use tile spacers or small pieces of cardboard to space the tiles temporarily while the adhesive sets. Grout all tiles in the usual way.

PLASTIC SEALING STRIP

This is an L-shaped plastic molding with a flexible blade along each edge that seals against the wall and against the tub (see pages 70–71). It forms a waterproof seal around a tub while covering small gaps between the wall and the edges of the tub. Some plastic sealing strips are self-adhesive; others need to be embedded in tile adhesive. In both cases, the tiles are set over the vertical half of the strip, although some types are designed so they can be installed later, when tiling is complete. That type simply is stuck to the face of the tiles.

Sinks

A small area of tiles behind a sink may be all that's needed to protect the wall from splashes. This is especially true if the sink doesn't happen to be in a bathroom or kitchen but is in another area of the house where a large area of tiles might be considered out of place.

Make sure to use tiles with glazed edges, at least around the edges of the backsplash because the edges will be visible. Or, you could use commercially available border tiles, tile trim, or even a painted wooden molding.

TOOLS: Tape measure, pencil, level, small trowel, notched adhesive spreader, grout spreader, sponge, bucket, clean cloth

MATERIALS: Tile adhesive, tiles, tile spacers, water

  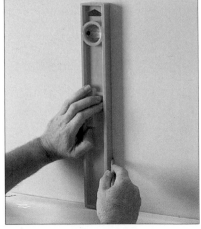

1 The sink already should be level, but you ought to make sure by checking with a level. Handle any slight deviation from horizontal by inserting additional cardboard spacers between the tiles and the sink (see Step 4). This irregular gap is concealed with silicone sealant. Measure the width of the sink, and mark the center point on the wall.

2 There's no need to make a gauge rod for a small job like this. You'll save yourself time if you simply use a wall tile to measure off the tile positions along the wall, making an allowance for the tile spacers. This will let you judge whether your starting point should be in line with the center of the sink or offset to one side of center by half a tile.

3 After determining the best starting point, use a level to draw a vertical guideline on the wall. Extend this line to the top of the finished backsplash. If the sink has a flat surface next to the wall, there's no need for a horizontal piece of wood; just tile directly from the top of the sink. Similarly, with such a small area of tiles, there's no need for a vertical furring strip either.

POSITIONING THE TILES

A backsplash behind a sink is always made up of whole tiles. Small tiles are a better choice than large ones because they're more in scale with the sink.

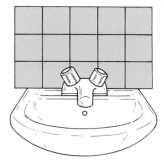

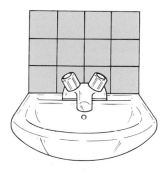

You can vary both the height and width to suit your needs, but make the tiled area at least 12 inches tall to protect the wall from water splashes. You may want to make it even higher if it's going to be a background for a mirror or shelves.

Depending on the size of your tiles, you can make a small backsplash by tiling up to the edges of the sink only (left). Or, you could arrange your tiles to extend beyond the edges of the sink at each side (right). Moving the starting point by half a tile to one side of the sink's center point may be enough to let you do this.

4 Spread adhesive to one side of the guideline, and begin tiling toward the edge of the sink. Set the tiles slightly above the sink on cardboard spacers. When you've tiled half of the backsplash, work in the other direction to finish it. Grout the tiles as usual, but leave the gap between the bottom row of tiles and sink for now. You'll use silicone sealant here.

TILING ABOVE A SHAPED SINK

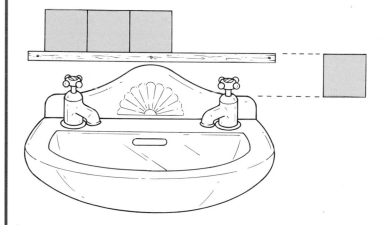

If the top of the sink isn't flat, use a furring strip above the highest point to support the whole tiles that form the backsplash. From the lowest point of the sink top, measure vertically up the wall the distance of one tile's height. Don't forget to factor in an allowance for the tile grout in your measurement. Temporarily nail a horizontal furring strip to the wall at this point. Tile above the wood using whole tiles. When the adhesive is set, remove the wood and fill in with cut tiles.

Tubs

A backsplash around a tub might extend around two or even three sides and probably will require cutting tiles unless it extends beyond the tub at one or both ends. If you'd rather keep the backsplash the same as the tub's dimensions and the tub is flanked by two walls, you should tile toward the inside corner, cutting tiles to fit together in the corner. If the tub is bordered by three walls, treat the back wall as you would any other (tiling out from the center with equal-size cut tiles at both ends) and begin tiling the end walls with whole tiles, working in toward the back wall. Use the same technique to tile a kitchen backsplash.

TOOLS: Sealant dispenser, tape measure, pencil, hacksaw, small trowel, notched adhesive spreader, glass cutter or tile spike, steel rule, tile file, grout spreader, sponge, clean cloth, bucket

MATERIALS: Tissue paper, silicone bath sealant, plastic sealing strip, tiles, tile adhesive, tile spacers, grout, water

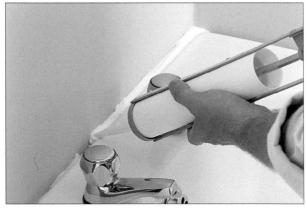

1 Where a tub is set in the corner of the room, you may find that the walls aren't at an exact right angle to each other, which will cause a tapered gap between one side of the tub and the wall. In this situation, make sure that the long side of the tub is tight against the wall; the gap along the short side will be easier to conceal. A very slight gap might even be hidden by the thickness of the tiles and adhesive themselves, but any larger gap probably will need to be covered with a commercially available sealing strip. Make sure that the tub is level before you start work.

2 To make doubly sure that water won't be able to penetrate the tiles and run down behind the tub, before you add the sealing strip and tiles, fill the gap with silicone sealant. If the gap is wide, you may have a hard time getting the sealant to fill it; the bead of sealant will just fall through. In this case, simply wedge some crumpled tissue paper into the gap before you apply the sealant. This will help fill the gap and provide some support for the sealant. Apply a thick bead of sealant, adding a bit extra in the corner where the ends of the sealing strip will meet.

ARRANGING THE TILES

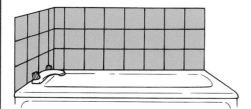

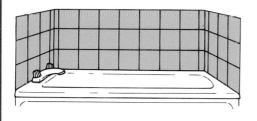

How you arrange the cut tiles on a backsplash for a tub will depend on how many walls you have to deal with.

If the backsplash is L-shaped, start with a whole tile at each end and work toward the inside corner, where any cuts should be made (left). If the backsplash extends around three sides, tile the back wall as usual with equal-size cut tiles at each end. Then, on the ends, work from whole tiles toward the inside corners.

ACRYLIC TUBS

If you're tiling around a newer acrylic tub, fill the tub with water before you set the tiles on the wall and seal around the edges. That way, if the bath happens to expand or contract, it will be much less likely to break the seal. In fact, this is a good idea with any type of tub.

3 Some sealing strips have a self-adhesive backing. Simply peel off the protective paper and press the strip against the wall so that its flexible blade makes a good seal with the top of the tub. Miter the ends where they meet in the corner, adding more silicone sealant if necessary to ensure a watertight joint. If the strip isn't self-adhesive, just embed it in the tile adhesive.

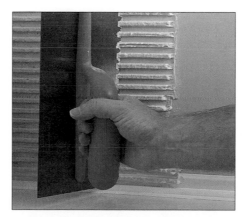

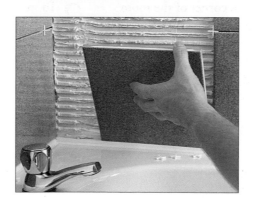

4 After laying out the backsplash and deciding on a starting point, spread a layer of adhesive onto the wall. Work on a small area at a time so the adhesive will stay workable. Make sure that it completely covers the sealing strip.

5 Add the tiles, working toward the corner if the tub is bordered by two walls. Make sure the tiles are embedded securely, and add tile spacers for uniform grout gaps. Grout the tiles in the usual way.

Countertops

Despite the variety of laminated kitchen countertops, tiling remains one of the best ways to give this hardworking area a tough, cleanable surface. In addition, tile offers a wide range of colors, patterns, and textures designed to help you add style and personality to your kitchen. As you shop for tile, remember that standard ceramic wall tiles won't work on countertops: They're not strong enough to withstand heat from pots and pans and the kind of wear that a kitchen countertop routinely gets. Instead, use special tiles designed for this purpose. If you'd like the backsplash and countertop to match, use the same tiles on the wall. Also make sure you use an epoxy-type grout designed for use in kitchens.

TOOLS: Hammer, saw, small trowel, notched adhesive spreader, wooden straightedge, tape measure, felt-tip pen, tile cutter, filling knife, plastic scouring pad, sponge, bucket

MATERIALS: Wooden molding, nails, tile adhesive, tiles, epoxy grout, water

PLANNING AND LAYING OUT

Although you can give an existing countertop a facelift with tile, it's usually best to start with a fresh surface. Use marine-grade plywood that's at least ½ inch thick. If you plan to install it on your existing cabinets, you won't need to provide extra support; otherwise, reinforce the plywood by screwing battens to the underside, around the edges, and across its width at about 24-inch intervals.

Where possible, adjust the width and length of the plywood so you won't have to cut any tiles. If you do have to cut some tiles to fit, use a tile cutter. Countertop tiles are too hard to break by scoring and snapping with hand tools. Often, you can rent a tile cutter at a local rental store or tile retailer.

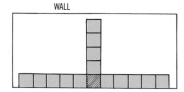

Straight countertop
If you're tiling a straight countertop and it's set against a back wall only, begin in the center front. If necessary, insert equal-size cut tiles at each end.

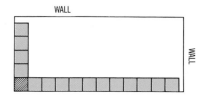

Top bounded by two walls
If the countertop is straight, begin with a whole tile at the front corner and work toward each wall, filling in with cut tiles at the walls as necessary.

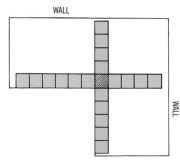

L-shaped countertop
Begin with a whole tile at the corner of the two surfaces. Work toward each end and the walls.

LAYING THE TILES

1 Begin by attaching the wooden molding around the countertop so its height matches the thickness of the tiles. If you plan to stain the molding, do so before laying the tiles.

Spread adhesive on the countertop using the notched spreader. Cover an area of no more than 1 square yard at a time.

Lay the tiles, using pieces of cardboard no more than ⅛ inch thick for spacers. Some countertop tiles come in panels on a mesh backing and are already spaced. With this type, you'll need to make sure that each tile is firmly embedded in the adhesive by pressing down with a grout spreader or similar tool.

2 Periodically check that the tiles are level by holding a wooden straightedge across them. Any tiles that are too high or too low should carefully be lifted and set in fresh adhesive.

3 Insert cut tiles where the countertop meets the wall. If you're left with too small a gap to fill, you can conceal it with decorative wooden molding.

GROUTING

When tiling a kitchen countertop, you'll need to use a two-part epoxy grout. It's not only waterproof and stain-resistant, but it's also hygienic and resistant to germs. It's important to work quickly when you're using epoxy grout because it hardens so fast and can be so difficult to remove from the faces of tiles.

1 Epoxy grout is much stiffer than normal grout and must be applied in a different way. Apply it directly to the joints with a filling knife.

2 As soon as you've filled all the joints, gently clean the surface of the tiles with a wet plastic kitchen scouring pad. This will remove any residue from the tiles and smooth the grout between them. Keep the pad flat so you won't run the risk of dragging any of the grout from the joints.

Finally, sponge off the surface of the tiles, then let the grout harden for the specified amount of time before using the countertop.

Mosaics and Marbles

Mosaics are much smaller than normal wall tiles, usually only 1 to 2 inches square. Because of this, they often come on sheets, either on a mesh backing or with a paper facing. The size of the sheet will vary depending on the size of the individual tiles. Mosaic tiles may be made of glazed ceramic or glass.

Although you can use mosaics just as you would standard wall tiles, they're usually best reserved for small areas such as backsplashes since their small size makes a large area look too busy. But because of their small size, they're perfect for tiling curved surfaces; you can easily wrap the sheets around a curve without the joints between the tiles opening up too much.

Marble tiles are much more expensive than regular ceramic tiles, but they bring a unique quality to a tiled surface. They're completely flat, with flush-grouted joints that create a smooth, elegant finish.

Laying out mosaics

The technique for laying out mosaics is essentially the same as for any wall tiles. As before, for a large area, you'll want to make a gauge rod that's marked off in panel widths and lengths. It's important to remember that you can cut strips of mosaics from the sheets to fill in at the ends of rows, but because the individual tiles are so small, you may not be able to cut the tiles themselves.

TOOLS: Tape measure, pencil, level

MATERIALS: Mosaic sheets

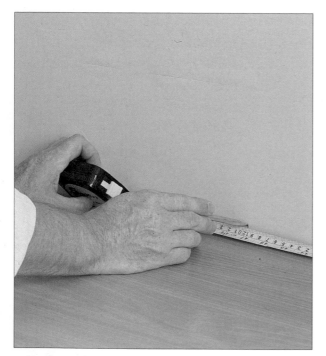

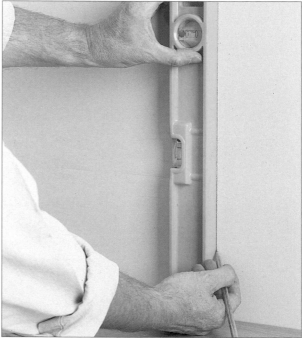

1 Measure to find the center of the area to be tiled and mark the point with a pencil. Although you can use mosaics to tile an entire wall, these small tiles look best on smaller areas, such as this backsplash behind a kitchen countertop. Because the countertop already should be level, you can work directly from it rather than using a support batten.

2 Use a level to extend the pencil mark vertically up the wall. Make the line the full height of the backsplash you'll be tiling. Ideally, it should come out equal to a multiple of whole sheets; if it doesn't, then at least make it a multiple of whole tiles. If the backsplash is between a countertop and upper cabinets, locate any cut tiles at the very top where they'll be concealed.

3 If you're tiling a small area like this wall behind a countertop, there's no need to make a gauge rod; simply use a sheet of mosaics to mark the tile positions along the wall. Remember to allow for the correct spacing between sheets; it should match the spacing between the tiles on the sheet.

4 At each end, you may find you only need part of a sheet to finish tiling, possibly with a row of cut tiles in the corner. Because of their small size, any cut tiles should be at least half a tile wide. The gap shown here is too narrow to fill easily; cutting the thin slivers of tile would be too difficult.

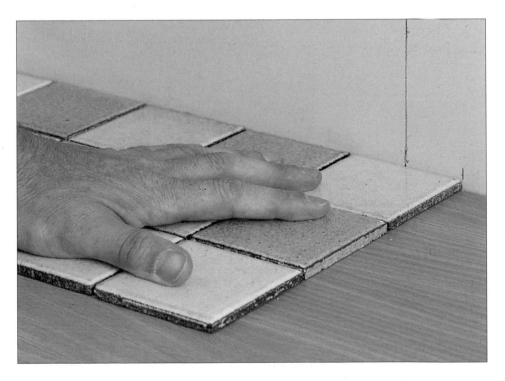

5 To get around having narrow cut tiles at each end of the backsplash, reposition the starting point by half a tile to one side and draw a new vertical line. There's no need to use a vertical wooden guide when tiling a backsplash, especially with sheets of mosaics, but for a larger area, you may want to nail one in place temporarily.

Setting mosaics

The techniques used for setting mosaic sheets to the wall are similar to those used for ordinary tiles. However, you must be especially careful to make sure that all of the individual tiles are embedded firmly in the adhesive. Since the tiles are small, pressing each one into the adhesive isn't practical. A much more effective solution is to use a grout spreader or a wooden tamping block, working the tool across each sheet with a firm slapping motion and pressing down several tiles with each blow.

The correct spacing between sheets also is important; it must match the spacing between the tiles on the sheet. Use pieces of cardboard of the appropriate thickness to help achieve the correct spacing.

TOOLS: Small trowel, notched adhesive spreader, grout spreader, plasterer's trowel, level, long wooden straightedge

MATERIALS: Mosaic sheets, tile adhesive, cardboard for spacers

1 After determining the starting point, spread adhesive on the wall—enough to set three or four sheets of mosaic tiles.

2 Press the first sheet of tiles into the adhesive, aligning its side edge carefully with the vertical pencil line.

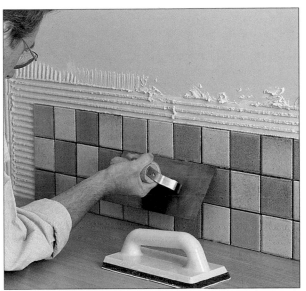

3 Use a float-type grout spreader to embed the tiles in the adhesive, working across the sheet with a slapping motion and delivering light but firm blows. This also will ensure that the mesh backing is stretched out fully, so the gaps between the tiles will be uniform.

4 Be careful to keep the sheets aligned so the horizontal joints are continuous. One way of checking the alignment is to hold the edge of a plasterer's trowel against the underside of each row of tiles, pressing upward lightly if necessary to bring the sheets into alignment.

ARRANGING THE SHEETS

Sheets of mosaics often are made up of tiles in several different colors that are arranged in a random pattern.

With very small mosaics, this may be truly random—in fact, each sheet may be different than the next. But with larger mosaics, the tiles may be arranged in the same pattern on each sheet or, in each box, there may be sheets with two or three different patterns. It's worth checking for this; the sheets may look better one way than another.

You might want to take the extra trouble of laying out several sheets on the floor. Even with a random arrangement of tiles, you should try to give the finished wall a balanced appearance.

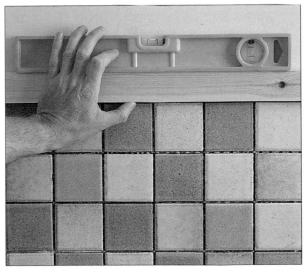

5 After setting two horizontal rows of sheets, use a level and long wooden straightedge to check that they're level and in line. Make any necessary adjustments. Continue adding sheets this way until you've covered most of the wall.

Cutting in

The small size of mosaics means that in many cases you won't have to cut tiles at the ends of rows to complete the job. However, if you can't avoid cutting tiles, you'll have to remove them individually from the sheets, measure the gaps to be filled, then cut the tiles to fit. With larger mosaics, you may find that a combination wheel cutter/snapper works best; by the same token, scoring the tile and breaking off the waste with a pair of nippers works best for smaller mosaics.

TOOLS: Crafts knife, notched adhesive spreader, tape measure, felt-tip pen, steel rule; glass cutter, tile spike and nippers, or wheel cutter/snapper

MATERIALS: Mosaic sheets, tile adhesive

1 When you reach the end of the backsplash, cut individual strips of tiles from the sheets as needed to fill the remaining gap. Place the sheet facedown and cut through the mesh backing with a sharp crafts knife.

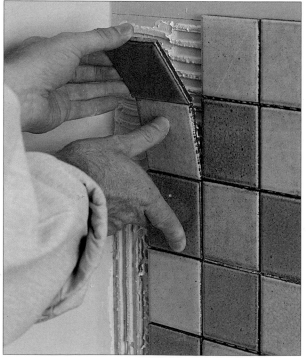

2 Remove any projecting paper backing from the strips of tiles. Then spread a layer of adhesive on the wall and press the tiles in place, embedding them firmly and aligning them carefully with all adjacent tiles.

CROOKED TILES

Occasionally you'll find that a tile on the sheet is out of place or crooked. If you notice this before you set the sheet on the wall, you can cut the tile out and set it separately. If you don't notice the crooked tile until after the sheet is on the wall, you'll have to free the tile from its backing and twist it into line.

1 If a tile is noticeably crooked after you've set a sheet, cut through the backing on all four sides with a sharp crafts knife.

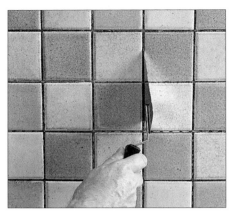

2 Being careful not to knock the tile off the wall, use a small trowel to push the tile gently back into line with its neighbors.

3 If you need to cut some tiles to fill in remaining spaces, remove them individually from the sheet. Measure and mark them as you would a normal-size tile, then score and snap them or nibble off the waste.

4 Press the individual cut tiles in place to fill the remaining gap in the corner. Since their spacing won't be fixed by the sheet of mesh backing, you'll need to add the appropriate spacers, such as pieces of cardboard.

Grouting

As with all tiles, the joints between mosaics need grouting. But because the individual tiles are so much smaller and there are so many more joints, shaping them could be a time-consuming chore. And, you might even find the grout starts to harden before you finish.

    As a result, after applying the grout, it's better just to sponge the mosaics and leave the grout flush with the edges of the tiles. Since the tiles usually are beveled slightly to produce a V-shaped joint, you'll get neat joints with very little effort.

TOOLS: Small trowel, grout spreader, sponge, soft cloth, bucket

MATERIALS: Grout, water

1 Scoop up some grout with a small trowel and press it onto the face of the mosaic. Spread it with the grout spreader, pressing it into the joints. Hold the blade of the spreader at an angle, working it diagonally across the joints to ensure that they're full, but keeping as much grout as possible off the faces of the tiles.

2 Wipe the tiles with a damp sponge to remove the excess grout and smooth the joints. Rinse the sponge often in clean water. Be careful, however, not to drag grout from the joints by pressing too hard. When the grout is completely dry, polish the powdery film from the faces of the tiles with a soft, clean cloth.

PAPER-FACED MOSAICS

1 Some small mosaics, such as these glass tiles, have a paper facing sheet that holds them together instead of a mesh backing. They're set on the wall exactly the same way as mesh-backed types, and are embedded by slapping with a grout spreader. After allowing the adhesive to dry, soak the paper facings of the mosaic sheets with a wet sponge. Make sure that each sheet of paper is soaked completely and thoroughly.

2 Wait a few minutes for the water to soak into the paper, then peel off each sheet.

3 Clean the tiles with a sponge and clean water to remove all traces of the paper adhesive. Then spread grout over the mosaic panels, making sure you fill all the joints. Using a sponge to remove excess grout can drag it from the joints; instead, it's better to let it dry slightly, then wipe off the excess with a damp cloth. When the grout is completely dry, it's time to polish the tiles in the normal way.

Marble tiles

Although marble tiles are set on the wall much like ceramic tiles, there are some important points to consider if you want to get good results. Marble tiles are perfectly flat with square-cut edges and look best if set with very narrow joints between them. In addition, they're translucent so any irregular coloring of the wall behind them shows through pale-colored tiles. Finally, although marble isn't difficult to cut, it's best to use a tile cutter rather than a glass cutter or tile spike and trying to snap them by hand. That's because marble tiles don't always cut as cleanly as ceramic tiles, and the tile cutter will give you a better cut. You can easily clean up cut edges with silicone carbide sandpaper.

TOOLS: Paintbrush, tape measure, pencil, level, gauge rod, small trowel, notched adhesive spreader, grout spreader, sponge, clean cloth, bucket, felt-tip pen, tile cutter

MATERIALS: Sealer, white water-based paint; furring strips, masonry nails, marble tiles, tile adhesive, grout, water

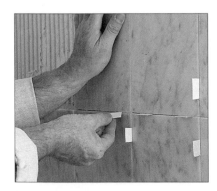  

1 After laying out the wall and attaching furring strips as guides, begin to set the marble tiles the same way you would set ceramic tiles. Once again, they'll look best if the joints between them are as thin as possible—about ¹⁄₁₆ inch—so instead of using conventional tile spacers, insert pieces of thin cardboard.

2 You can treat external corners the same way you would treat ceramic tiles by overlapping the edges, but for best results, the edges of the tiles should be mitered. Many tile suppliers will miter the tiles for you; if not, though, you can use a tablesaw with a diamond-tipped blade to do the job yourself.

3 As with other forms of tiling, complete the main wall first, then the return wall, working away from the external corner. Position the corner tiles carefully, inserting thin pieces of cardboard between the mitered faces to maintain the correct spacing. This will leave a neat joint at the point of the corner.

4 Because they're perfectly flat, it's important that the faces of the tiles are flush. Otherwise, you'll botch the job. As you work, periodically hold a wooden straightedge across the faces of the tiles to check for any individual slabs that are too high or too low.

5 If necessary, carefully remove any of the tiles that are out of line, scrape off the old adhesive, and apply a fresh coat to the back of the tile (not the wall). Refit the tile in its space and use the straightedge to check that it's completely level with the surrounding tiles.

6 When you begin to grout the tiles, fill the joints of the external corners first. Hold the grout spreader at an angle and with a little grout on the edge of the blade, press it gently into the corner joint. Then gently draw the blade up the corner to scrape off any excess.

7 Grout the rest of the tiles in the usual way, working the blade of the spreader diagonally across the joints rather than along them to prevent any of the grout from being accidentally dragged out of the joints.

8 Because the grout must be flush with the tiles, don't use a sponge to wash off the excess. Wait for it to harden slightly, then wipe off the excess with a cloth. Try to keep grout off the faces of the tiles when grouting.

PAINTING THE WALL

When sealing the wall before tiling, it's a good idea to mix the sealer with white water-based paint if you'll be putting up pale-colored tiles. This will prevent any dark-colored areas on the wall from showing through the tiles once they're in place.

Dilute the sealant according to manufacturer's instructions, then add the white paint, mixing it with between one quarter and half as much paint as sealer. Apply the mixture to the wall and let it dry completely.

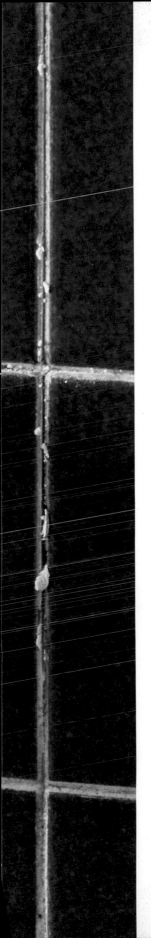

Renovation and Repair

Tiles provide a long-lasting surface that's easy to clean and will keep its good looks for many years. However, as with any decorative finish, time takes its toll on the appearance of tile. Grout becomes stained and discolored—even if the tiles are regularly cleaned—and the tiles themselves crack or become broken from accidental knocks.

When redecorating a kitchen or bath, you may find you're left with unsightly screw holes in tiles where wall-mounted fixtures have been removed and not replaced. Or you may have inherited a tiled surface that was in poor condition when you bought your house. Although there's not much you can do about poor quality and uneven tiling short of tearing it out and starting over, you can replace grout that's seen better days and tiles that have become damaged. Both jobs are easy to do and are well worth the effort. They can make your tiles look like new.

This chapter contains

Renewing grout

Over the years, grout becomes discolored and stained, particularly where the tiles are subjected to a lot of moisture, such as in a shower or around a bathtub. If ventilation is poor, the grout lines take a long time to dry out. Eventually, this leads to the growth of black mold, which is especially hard to remove.

Fortunately, it's an easy situation to correct. Essentially, all you need to do is rake out all of the old grout and replace it. Replacing the grout makes even an old tiled surface look new again.

TOOLS: Grout raker, small trowel, grout spreader, sponge, grout shaper, clean cloth, bucket

MATERIALS: Grout, water

1 Use a grout raker or an awl to remove the old grout from around the tiles, being careful not to damage their edges. Do all the vertical joints, then the horizontal joints (or vice versa) so you don't miss any. Make sure you remove the grout down to at least half the thickness of the tile.

2 Press some fresh grout onto the face of the tiles with a small trowel, then spread it over the tiles, pressing it into the joints. Move the spreader diagonally over the joints rather than along them to prevent the grout from being dragged out again. Continue until all the joints have been filled.

3 Use a wet sponge to wash all excess grout from the faces of the tiles, but don't press too hard or you may remove it from the joints, too. Then allow the grout to harden slightly.

4 Run a grout shaper along the joints to give them the right profile, or use a large-diameter wooden dowel. Use a wet sponge to remove any grout that might squeeze out.

CLEANING FLUIDS

You can remove minor stains and fungal growth from grout using a commercially available grout cleaner. It contains a variety of cleaners and biological agents to clean the grout and discourage further mold growth.

The normal procedure is to dilute the cleaner with an equal amount of warm water, then apply it to the grout with a brush or a sponge. After you've allowed the fluid to dry, simply rinse off any residue and dry the tiles with an absorbent cloth.

5 Let the grout dry, then polish off the powdery film from the faces of the tiles with a soft, clean cloth.

IDEAL TOOLS

Grout is designed to provide a hard filling for the joints between tiles, so it takes a little effort to remove. Although you may be able to improvise a tool for the job, be very careful not to damage the tiles themselves. An ordinary awl can work well, but its depth of penetration can be difficult to control. The best bet is a grout raker with short teeth designed specifically for the job. Grout rakers come in various forms. The multi-toothed type on the left has a thin blade that works well for narrow joints; the tool on the right handles wider joints and is used to score tiles before cutting them.

Replacing a damaged tile

Over the years, ceramic wall tiles can become damaged from accidental blows. Or, you may find that changing bathroom or kitchen fixtures has left some tiles with unsightly screw holes that can't easily be filled or concealed.

This kind of damage easily spoils the appearance of a tiled surface and, where the tiles are used as a backsplash or surround for a tub or shower, allows water to penetrate to the wall behind with potentially damaging results. In a kitchen, a cracked or broken tile on a countertop work surface traps dirt and germs.

Fortunately, replacing a damaged tile is a straightforward repair that you can easily do yourself.

TOOLS: Grout raker, electric drill, ceramic tile/masonry bit, cold chisel, hammer, thick gloves, goggles, small trowel, notched adhesive spreader, wooden straightedge, grout spreader, sponge, grout shaper, clean cloth, bucket

MATERIALS: Tile, tile adhesive, tile spacers, grout, water

IDEAL TOOL
A ceramic tile drill bit is designed to bite immediately into the glaze of a tile without skidding, thereby eliminating the need to use masking tape or to break the glaze with a sharp, pointed tool. You'll find ceramic tile bits available in all the most popular sizes.

1 In this example, a tile is being replaced where a wall-mounted fixture was removed, exposing two unsightly screw holes. The first job is to completely rake out the grout on all four sides of the tile.

2 Drill a series of holes around the center of the tile using a ceramic tile bit and an electric drill. Since the tile will be removed, you could even use a masonry bit without tape; it won't matter if the bit skips.

3 Use a hammer and cold chisel to cut through the tile between the holes, and chop out the center of the tile. Wear thick work gloves to protect your hands and goggles to shield your eyes from the sharp fragments of tile that will fly out.

4 Work carefully toward the edges of the tile, gently breaking away pieces. Be especially careful when you get close to another tile; a slip could mean replacing more than one. When the tile is out, chisel out as much adhesive as you can.

5 Check that you've removed enough adhesive by inserting the dry replacement tile and noting how it sits in relation to the surrounding tiles: It can't protrude above their surfaces. Then coat the back of the tile with adhesive and set it in place.

A SUITABLE REPLACEMENT

Finding an exact replacement for a broken tile can be a problem unless you happen to have some spares left from the original tiling job. This is another good reason always to buy more tiles than you actually need for a given project; you'll have extras to keep on hand for the inevitable repairs.

If the tiles are old or you don't know their source or manufacturer, you may not be able to find an exact match. In this case, the best you can do is look for an inset tile of the same size to drop in and perhaps remove a few other tiles at random to install others like it. That way, your repair won't be as obvious and you can give your tiles a new look at the same time.

Or, you could remove several tiles around the broken one and insert picture tiles or a tiled panel of some sort. Although all of these options are a lot of work, they're probably your only choices if you can't find exact replacements.

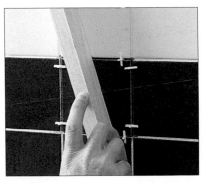

6 Press the tile into place with a wooden straightedge. This will make sure the tile is flush with the adjacent tiles. Insert tile spacers for uniform grout joints. When the adhesive has set, remove the spacers and grout the tile in the usual way.

Glossary

Biscuit

The clay body of a tile to which a liquid ceramic glaze is applied. The tile is then fired under intense heat in a kiln to set the glaze into a hard surface. Patterned tiles may be fired several times, with each part of the pattern added separately.

Border tile

A tile designed specifically for edging an area of tiles. They're usually narrower than standard tiles, may be colored or patterned, and their outer edges are glazed for a neat finish.

Corner trim

A molded plastic strip designed for finishing an external corner where two tiled walls meet. Corner trim is essential when using tiles with unglazed edges. It comes in various colors and sizes to accommodate different thicknesses of tile.

Cutting in

Cutting tiles to fit a narrow gap at the end of a row (where it meets an adjacent wall, for example). Cut tiles should be at least half a tile wide. This creates a neater appearance and avoids cutting thin slivers of tile.

Dado

A horizontal row of tiles or a wooden molding that runs across a wall at waist height. Dadoes are used to break up large expanses of tile or provide a break between different tiling layouts.

Field tiles

Standard, uncut tiles used to fill the center portion of a tiled area.

Gauge rod

A wooden batten marked off at intervals that correspond to the width of the tiles being used (with an allowance for grout joints). It's used to determine where the horizontal and vertical rows of tiles will fall on the wall and to show the width of any cut tiles at the ends of rows. It also helps determine the best point to begin tiling.

Grout

Fills the joints between tiles, providing a hard surface. Some grouts are completely waterproof; epoxy grout also is hygienic and safe for use on kitchen counters.

Grout raker

A rigid-bladed tool for scraping out old cracked and discolored grout before regrouting or removing a damaged tile.

Grout shaper

A plastic tool used to neatly shape grout joints while the grout is still soft.

Insert

A small square tile inserted at the point where the corners of four larger tiles would normally meet.

Inset tile

A standard-size tile with a central motif used to provide visual interest in a large expanse of single-colored tiles. Insets can be used at random throughout a tiled area or in a specific pattern.

Laying out

Marking the wall with the starting point for tiling and attaching guide battens (if necessary). Normally, you begin tiling at the center of the wall and work toward the ends.

Mitered

Cut at an angle of 45 degrees. The adjacent ends of border tiles, for example, are mitered when they frame a backsplash. This way the pattern continues on all sides.

Mosaics

Small tiles in sheet form with a mesh backing or paper facing.

Nippers

Used to break off small bits of waste when making a cutout in a tile or removing a narrow strip. Special narrow-jawed nippers are available for working in confined spaces.

Pencil tile

A very narrow tile, not much wider than a pencil, with a rounded face normally used along with dado tiles.

Picture tiles

Groups of tiles that fit together to make a larger picture. They can be used much like an inset to break up a large expanse of tiles.

Profile gauge

A special tool for copying the shapes of objects and transferring them to tiles for cutting.

Quarter-round tile

A narrow rounded tile for use at the junction of a tiled backsplash and a tub or sink.

Reveal

The narrow return strips of a wall around a recessed window.

Squeegee

The tool used for spreading grout.

Template

A pattern (normally paper) used to copy the shape of an object and transfer it to a tile for cutting.

Tile file

A special file for cleaning up the edges of tiles after they've been cut. Some have both flat and curved faces, allowing for straight and curved cuts.

Tile scorer

A tool with a narrow, hardened, chisel-like blade for scoring the glaze of a tile before snapping it in two. Without a tile scorer (or a glass cutter), it's impossible to get a clean, straight break.

Tile spike

A pencil-like version of the tile scorer with a needlelike tip. Easier to use than the chisel type, since its tip is able to better follow the edge of a steel rule for greater accuracy when scoring.

Index

Meredith® Press
An imprint of Meredith® Books

Do-It-Yourself Decorating
Step-by-Step Decorating: Wall Tiling
Editor, Shelter Books: Denise L. Caringer
Contributing Editor: David A. Kirchner
Contributing Designer: Jeff Harrison
Copy Chief: Angela K. Renkoski

Meredith® Books
Editor in Chief: James D. Blume
Managing Editor: Christopher Cavanaugh
Director, New Product Development: Ray Wolf
Vice President, Retail Sales: Jamie L. Martin

Meredith Publishing Group
President, Publishing Group: Christopher M. Little
Vice President and Publishing Director: John P. Loughlin

Meredith Corporation
Chairman of the Board and Chief Executive Officer: Jack D. Rehm
President and Chief Operating Officer: William T. Kerr
Chairman of the Executive Committee: E. T. Meredith III

First published 1996 by Haynes Publishing
© Haynes Publishing 1996. All rights reserved.

This edition published by Meredith Corporation, Des Moines Iowa, 1997
Printed in France
Printing Number and Year: 5 4 3 2 1 00 99 98 97 96
Library of Congress Catalog Card Number: 96-78038
ISBN: 0-696-20681-1